Words, Words, Words

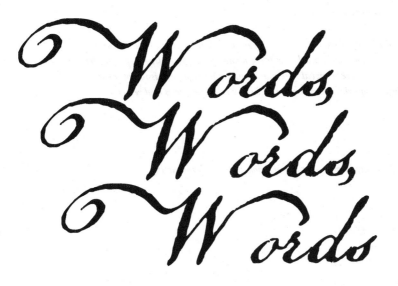

Words, Words, Words

MOSTLY ESSAYS ON THE ENGLISH LANGUAGE AND LITERATURE

GLYNN BAUGHER

WORDS, WORDS, WORDS
MOSTLY ESSAYS ON THE ENGLISH LANGUAGE AND LITERATURE

iUniverse books may be ordered through booksellers or by contacting:

iUniverse
1663 Liberty Drive
Bloomington, IN 47403
www.iuniverse.com
1-800-Authors (1-800-288-4677)

ISBN: 978-1-5320-9880-2 (sc)
ISBN: 978-1-5320-9881-9 (e)

Print information available on the last page.

iUniverse rev. date: 04/06/2020

PREFACE

Playacting at madness, Hamlet responds to a query from the garrulous toady Polonius: "What do you read, My Lord?"

"Words, words, words."

Indeed, that's about all that one can read, write, and speak. This book contains words about words—words about the peculiarities and beauties of the English language, including individual words, and words about the best of words in the best order—a few of the glories of our great literature, from the chortle per minute of the matchless P. G. Wodehouse to the high seriousness of the invented world of Yoknapatawpha County, William Faulkner's fiction that is often truer than history, the cosmos and microcosmos of the American South.

Most of these pieces were written when I was a Professor of English at Frostburg State University in Maryland, or not so long after my retirement—occasional pieces written for diverse occasions, ranging from needing a keynote address for the English Department's annual Colloquium of the best student writing; to contributing to a periodical publication of our university's writer's hotline, *Gramma*; to writing a text to use in my Word Study course; to a long, long paper on Irish literature in English and the literature of the American South for publication and a trans-Atlantic video teleconference celebrating the joint centenaries of Mary Immaculate College in Ireland and of Frostburg State University.

I hope that no one is shocked to discover that I am proud of these mostly small contributions, a few granules to add to the vast, expanding cone of knowledge about the English language and literature. Now in my 77th year, I THINK that my critical faculties are still intact, and I am pleased by the style as well as the content of these pieces. I enjoyed working with these again, and I trust that any generous reader can likewise find much to enjoy.

DEDICATION

I dedicate this book to those who were often the original audience for the writings: my colleagues at Frostburg State University.

Euphemistic Cursing

[This piece was written for oral presentation at the Torch Club of Cumberland, Maryland. Torch Clubs present professionals the opportunity to present talks on their professional interests to a mixed group.]

In his short story "Barn Burning," William Faulkner describes how Abner Snopes strikes his mules, "two savage blows with the peeled willow, but without heat . . . striking and reining back in the same movement." This is a rather apt figure of what euphemistic cursing is like: We strike out at the supernatural with verbal savagery but rein it in at the same time--just in case. Surely God cannot tell that W. C. Fields means to curse when he mutters Godfrey Daniel *sotto voce,* perhaps because he has to work with Baby Leroy again?

We use euphemisms mainly to talk about excretion, sex, death, and supernatural powers--to conceal the ugly, protect the prudish, or hide our fears. *Euphemism* derives from two Greek roots--*eu,* meaning "good," as in "sounding good," and *pheme,* "speech." We all use euphemisms and need them in everyday discourse. To avoid offense in social discourse is no great fault. Euphemistic cursing avoids offending our fellow creatures and perhaps supernatural powers also, again just in case. The Hebraic tradition considers profanity quite serious, the subject of the third of the ten Mosaic commandments. Of more worldly concern, euphemisms sometimes help to avoid the punishments of the Puritan blue laws, a 17th-century act of Parliament forbidding profanity in theatrical productions, or the Hollywood Production Code of 1930.

Social euphemisms are not so dishonest and reprehensible as is calling a lie that no one believes anymore *inoperative.* Some cultures seem to consider obscenity a greater fault than profanity; others think very little about casual obscenity but reprehend the profane severely. Obviously Dante revels in obscenity, but blasphemers are in the seventh circle of the Inferno with murderers and suicides. Chaucer likewise revels in bodily obscenity and always calls a fart a fart but severely reprehends those who rend God's bones with curses.

My subject is euphemistic profanity, not obscenity. *Profane* means "before" (that is, "outside") "the temple." Profanity attacks sacred belief to express surprise, exasperation, disgust, or anger. Let's consider some categories in which we humans curse euphemistically, often unaware of the origins of the expressions and their intent.

The simplest of curses (which word may be considered a generalized euphemism for "damns") is, of course, to damn someone or something. The simplest euphemism may be to find some alternative way to say "Damn it." Dang, darn, and drat are perhaps the most common. *Drat* is probably from "Odrat it," which we will return to later. To say "I'll be damned!" we resort to "I'll be jiggered/switched/dogged/blowed/blamed" (also used in "I can't get this blamed thing to work"). "Blast it all," I'll never get them all listed. The American South has a profusion of these, my favorite being, perhaps, the general euphemistic swear, gentle enough for the godliest granny, "Dog my cats."

To damn someone or something is to consign to hell, but direct mention of the Foe and infernal regions is also subject to euphemizing. Instead of *hell* we say *heck*, as in "What the heck is wrong?" H, E, double hockey-sticks. Or we say, "What in thunder . . .?" or "Go to blazes, or, especially the English, "Go to Halifax/Putney/Jericho/Guinea." In Victorian England, "Give them Jesse" meant "Give them hell," and "What in Sam Hill?" is still commonly known. The mention of hell was specifically forbidden by the Hollywood Production Code, so insistently that in the Brando movie from 1954 *The Wild Ones* the motorcycle gang that should have been called Hell's Angels was called the Black Rebels. Deuce(s) is used for both "damn" and Satan. "The deuce we are!" usually means "The devil/ the hell we are!" Another name for Satan, generalized as the Devil, is "the dickens." From an Old Norse word for "wizard" or "monster" we have the very old euphemism, Old Scratch, as my son named a diabolical cat we had, with double meaning. Sometimes we curse by a diametrically opposite linguistic twist, as Aeschylus shows that the Greeks appeased the Furies (the Erinyes) by calling them "the kindly ones" (the Eumenides). Thus, Satan is sometimes called "the good man" or "the great fellow."

In direct contrast to things infernal we often swear by general things made holy for the occasion, euphemizing as we go. The most contrary of these swearings is probably "Holy heck!"--just one in a line that contains "Holy cow/cats/hoptoads (valuable for the alliteration) /smoke (with its variant "Holy H. Smoke") /snakes/bilge water/ and "Holy Egypt" (one supposes for the Mosaic connection).

In Christendom, especially in Roman Catholic Christendom, swearing by the saints and subsidiary figures of the faith has always seemed less risky than swearing by godhead itself. Still, we have always euphemized even this kind of swearing. For Pete's sake is scarcely perceived as a curse by the demure utterer of this phrase, which seems to bless, but it is uttered in exasperation and is an amelioration of a swearing by St. Peter, called down from the empyrean regions and domesticated and made diminutive. Shakespeare has many a character who swears Marry, a sanitized swearing by the Virgin, used even, anachronistically, by the characters in *Julius Caesar.* Holy jumping mother of Jesus is a particularly expansive swearing by Mary, but it seems to be a variant of some Jesus swears we will hear anon. More swearing by Mary and by the saints doubtless existed in earlier times, but we don't hear a great deal of this in our Protestant-dominated country. It is possible that by George is a swearing by St. George, but more likely that is a substitute for the name of God, as clearly by Godfrey is.

In Christianity swearing by Godhead itself seems less taboo than swearing by Jesus. A few swears, primarily those by the Lord, may apply to either of the two figures in the Trinity, and the Holy Ghost gets almost none of the best swears, none of the euphemistic ones occurring to me. Law/Laws/Lawd are, of course, alterations of Lord. Again, these are often heard in the American South--everything from lawsy me to lawdy, lawdy, lawdy to law sakes, land's sake alive, and land alive.

Bridging the gap to the hardcore stuff is swearing by God but gentling it down to I swan/I swan to goodness, both favorites of my very gentle sister-in-law. We have lots of euphemisms for God's name, starting with the classical by Jove or by Jupiter. The Irish begorrah, made laughably prevalent in movies, is of course a way of saying a euphemistic by God. More common today are the seemingly innocent euphemisms gosh/golly/golly Moses, quickly mutating into the less-innocent goldarn and goldang. It takes the crinkum-crankum voice of Walter Brennan to say goldern with feeling and authenticity. Other phrases use good to effect: Good God!--too raw for most occasions--morphs into good grief, immortalized by Charlie Brown, good gracious, good gravy, goodness sakes alive, gracious to Betsy, and other variants. Great, as in Great God!, is also substituted, as in great Scott, great Caesar, great Caesar's ghost, and great shakes. Gosh pulls heavy duty in phrases, from the transparent gosh-almighty to gosh-all-fishhooks/hemlock/Potomac, gosh-dang, gosh-durn, ohmigosh, by-guess-and-gosh, and goshwalader.

Of course, the great big curse by God is God damn, sanitized in the medieval Latin curses of excommunication ("*Maledicat Deus pater . . . .*"). Whether used as an actual curse, an exclamation of a smaller kind, or an adjectival intensifier, the phrase is quite old among English-speaking people, so common that Joan of Arc referred to the English soldiers she opposed as goddams or goddems. Joseph Pulitzer, it is reported, was fond of sticking the big curse in between syllables of other words, thus sanitizing it a bit: "The trouble with you is that you are too inde-goddamned-pendent." Godfrey Daniel, goldern, and others already mentioned are Hayes Code bypasses for the movies. Sometimes the big curse is just initialized--G. D.--and gets by. More often, it is sanitized in a cutesy-pie phrase that scarcely suggests the big curse: Dadgum and doggone are variants that seem quite Uncle Remusy. Others very folksy-sounding are odrabbit it and odrat it, where the initial letter of God is dropped and some critter-verb put in place of the damn. One of the most common euphemistic swearings by God is egad, innocent enough to be a favorite on *Sesame Street*: "Egad, it sounds like a job for Sherlock Hemlock."

Mostly antiquated and unused today, the euphemistic curses that use an altered form of the word God combined with images of the crucifixion of Jesus were once quite prevalent. The best known of these is probably zounds, which most students pronounce to rhyme with *bounds,* though it is an elision of by God's wounds, and should rhyme with *wounds.* Odsoons is a variant, as is odzooks or, more commonly, gadzooks, *hooks* apparently referring to the nails used in the crucifixion, though perhaps to the fingers or nails of Jesus. Chaucer makes it clear that swearing by all parts of the body of the crucified Jesus was common among blasphemers, everything from by goddes armes to by his nailes. Shakespeare uses many swears of this kind, most notably sblood and ods bodkin in *Hamlet,* "by God's little body." King John, of Magna Carta infamy, swore by Goddes eyes.

Swearing simply by Jesus or Christ shows several interesting phenomena. Perhaps it is not surprising that in Christendom these swears are more numerous than any other. They are also more linguistically inventive and often euphemistically more remote from the name, so it would seem that this kind of cursing, especially in Protestantism, is felt to be more taboo even than swearing by God. Swearing by Jesus often uses just the opening sound of the name: gee and all of its variants--Jee, Jeez, gee whiz, by jingo, geewhillikers, geewhittakers, geewhillikins, geewizards, geehollikins, gee-my-knee, and all of the Jiminy variants, many adding a C-word to get a version of Christ in there too: Jiminy Cricket, Jiminy Christmas/Criminy/Crackers. One surmise is that Gemini is from *Jesu domine,* but I think the initial-syllable explanation is most likely. Also in the gee- category are jeepers, jeepers-creepers, bejeepers, bejesus, bejeebers, and bejabbers.

Euphemistic swears using only Christ to springboard from are for cry- (and the speaker bethinks himself) -ing out loud, cripes, criky, cracky (as in by cracky), criminy, Christmas, Christopher Columbus, and--my favorite--G. Rover Cripes.

Linguistically the most inventive use the device of extending the name to mitigate the oath, perhaps also altering the name. Those who would euphemize know that longer is nearly always better. Thus we have Judas Priest, where we curse by Jesus while suggesting that we are cursing by someone much more deserving of a curse. Judas Christopher comes closer to the name. Extended names are numerous, some of the best-known being Jesus H. Christ, Jesus H. Particular Christ, Jesus Christ on a crutch, Jesus

H. Christ on a bicycle, Jesus Christ and his brother Harry, and, more comically, holy jumping Jesus. If the disaster calls for a very long expletive to keep from hardcore stuff, we can always elaborate: holy jumping Mother of Jesus, G. Rover Cripes, and Jesus H. Particular Christ and his brother Harry on a bicycle-built-for-two!

To be human is to euphemize. To be human is to curse, cuss, or swear. To be human is to curse euphemistically. Apparently we just have to do so, even when we don't know that that's what we're doing. Still, we may not be religious enough to blaspheme so very vigorously anymore.

Etched in Vitriol

[This paper was written for presentation as the keynote address for Frostburg State University's annual English Department Colloquium of the best student writing.]

From time to time some of my friends and I burden each other with confessions of guilty pleasures. We tacitly understand that such confessions must not be tossed back in the others' teeth as proof of defective taste or used later as a counterweight in moments of heated aesthetic debate. Then we can confess the guilty pleasure we take in some irredeemably trashy TV program--some bit of crap that any right-thinking person would know heralds the decline of western civilization. Or we uncover the soft place in our heart (and our head) for some wretched little movie best left to merciful oblivion, except in these moments of unburdening. Sometimes we confess how some undeniably great work of literature leaves us as unmoved as stone, how we prefer a distinctly minor work, one that you would think only the author's mother could love.

I am here to confess a guilty pleasure: I collect mean-spirited, back-stabbing, vitriolic remarks that writers make about other writers. Now I know it must seem gauche on this occasion when we honor good writing to dig up writers savaging other writers. How can I justify such a lack of decorum?

The most obvious answer is that the choices must display wit, the panache that evinces the love of language that is excuse enough for our remembering the impolite. Robert Louis Stevenson said of Matthew Arnold, "Poor Matt [and here is daring indeed, calling the redoubtable Matthew Arnold "Matt"], he's gone to heaven, no doubt--but he won't like God." We see at once the wit of mocking the arch-critic for the exquisite delicacy of his taste. Or when the drama critic George Jean Nathan says of playwright J. M. Barrie, the author of *Peter Pan*, that he is "a triumph of sugar over diabetes," we appreciate how easy the victory is.

But apart from wit, can we find other guilt-assuaging reasons to delight in writers' attacks on their fellows? Can we raise this wallowing in muck to an activity seemly for this honorable and honoring event? You probably suspect that I'm going to say "Yes." Well, I'm going to say "Yes, maybe."

Let's discern some rules of good writing for you writers. Let's begin high indeed--Herman Melville savaging Ralph Waldo Emerson: "I could readily see in Emerson, notwithstanding his merit, a gaping flaw. It was the insinuation that had he lived in those days when the world was made, he might have offered some valuable suggestions." Add to this Israel Zangwill's comment on GBS: "The way Bernard Shaw believes in himself is very refreshing in these atheistic days when so many people believe in no God at all." From these two drops of vitriol, let's extrapolate Rule #1 of good writing: Have no high opinion of your own infallibility.

Still, Rule #2 says Have some intellectual substance. If not, you will be attacked as Jacqueline Susann (to sink low indeed) was attacked by Gloria Steinem: She is "for the reader who has put away comic books but isn't ready yet for editorials in the *Daily News* [a distinctly low-brow tabloid]." Likewise Katherine Mansfield on E. M. Forster: "[He] never gets any further than warming the teapot. He's a rare fine hand at that. Feel this teapot. Is it not beautifully warm? Yes, but there ain't going to be no tea." And Thomas Carlyle, the Scottish curmudgeon who had nastier things to say about more writers than perhaps anybody else, said of Samuel Taylor Coleridge, "Never did I see such apparatus got ready for thinking, and so little thought. He mounts scaffolding, pulleys, and tackle, gathers all the tools in the neighborhood with labor, with noise, demonstration, precept, abuse, and sets--three bricks." So have some intellectual substance, or else you'll be forgotten like Samuel Taylor Coleridge.

John Simon writes, "With *States of Shock* Sam Shepard appears to have finally attained what he was aiming at all along: total incomprehensibility." And though what Alice B. Toklas says of Gertrude Stein is meant as admiration, let's toss that in: "Gertrude has said things tonight it will take her ten years to understand." More to the point is Nora Joyce's remark to her husband James, "Why don't you write books people can read?" Thus the caveat to Have some intellectual substance is Rule #3, Be comprehensible.

However, comprehensibility has its price. Robert Morley suggests that Bertolt Brecht was so comprehensible he was simple-minded: "Brecht has not only never had an original thought, he takes twice as long as the average playgoer to have any thought at all." Rule #4: Be original.

But don't be so original that you don't write English. Rule #5, Use natural language. Mark Twain of Sir Walter Scott: "Did he know how to write English and didn't do it because he didn't want to?" Let's call on Mr. T to corroborate Mark Twain. I pity the fool who won't grant that Mr. T is a writer. He's as much a writer as Nora Joyce. I need his help to make this point. Mr. T says, "I don't do Shakespeare. I don't talk in that kind of broken English." If you don't use natural language, you might end up like Shakespeare.

Natural language suggests Rule #6, perhaps just a corollary of 5: Cultivate a simple English style, but have an ear. Richard Porson, though admiring Gibbon's *Decline and Fall of the Roman Empire* as the greatest work of English literature of the eighteenth century, said, "There could not be a better exercise for a schoolboy than to turn a page of it into English." Ford Madox Ford said of Joseph Conrad, "Conrad spent a day finding the *mot juste* and then killed it." Oscar Wilde on George Meredith: "His style is chaos, illumined by flashes of lightning. As a writer, he has mastered everything except language."

For Rule #7, let's call on Dorothy Parker and the 18th-century Duke of Gloucester. Parker on Theodore Dreiser: "The reading of [the novel] *Dawn* is a strain upon many parts, but the worst wear and tear fall upon the forearms." Gloucester, on having been presented the latest installment of Gibbon's *Decline and Fall*: "Another damned, thick, square book! Always scribble, scribble! Eh! Mr. Gibbon?" Rule #7 is Don't be so very prolix. Thus Clifton Fadiman criticizes Gertrude Stein: She "was a past master in making nothing happen very slowly."

Truman Capote gives us Rule #8, commenting on Jack Kerouac's continuous roll of paper that was the manuscript of *On the Road*: "That's not writing, that's typing." Rule #8, then is Polish your work.

Mary McCarthy says of Lillian Hellman, "Every word she writes is a lie, including *and* and *the*." Rule #9 is Be truthful.

Rule #10 is Don't call undue attention to yourself in your writing. If you follow this rule, you might not have it said of you as James Dickey said of Sylvia Plath that she was "the Judy Garland of American poetry." Or as Peter de Vries said of Emily Dickinson, "[She] was known to fly upstairs and hide in her room at the sound of callers. . . .Anything to be the center of attention."

Let's distill our last rule from the great fribble of English literature, Max Beerbohm. He said of D. H. Lawrence, "He never realized, don't you know—he never suspected that to be stark staring mad is somewhat of a handicap to a writer." Thus, our last rule, #11, is If you possibly can, be sane.

Ignore these rules at your peril. If you ignore them, you may have to suffer the fate of Emily Dickinson, James Joyce, and Joseph Conrad, the infamy of Gibbon and Shakespeare.

Psmith: the P Is Silent

[This piece was written for *Gramma*, a publication that ultimately grew out of Grammarphone, a writer's hotline at Frostburg State University.]

"As long as you're up anyway, Dad," says one of my daughters in the ingratiating tone reserved for turning a parent into a lackey, "would you get me the wor.SESS.ter.SHYER sauce out of the refrigerator?" What should I do--silently accept her egregious bias that spelling should indicate pronunciation? (Queen Elizabeth now pronounces the _t_ in often.) Or should I put on my dourest Mr. Dingledine-the-English-teacher look and say "It's WOOS.ter.sher or WUS.ter.sher or do without"?

Comic writers like P. G. Wodehouse (pronounced WOOD.house) know that readers reared on English eccentricity in the pronunciation of proper nouns will relish a character named Psmith, with a silent _p_ like ptarmigan. And if Worcester spells WOOS.ter and Leicester spells LES.ter, then inescapable logic tells us that the Wodehouse character the Earl of Blicester is a blister. The blackguard (BLAG.erd, called BLACK.GARD only by the linguistically backward) Stanley Featherstonehaugh Ukridge pronounces his middle name FETH.er.stun.au and his last name as YOOK.ridge, and who can argue?

Can we unscrew the inscrutable here? Why should the Norman name Cholmondeley be rendered as CHUM.lee? Why is the English poet Thomas Carew called KARE.ee but the American baseballer Rod Carew called ka.RUE? What song the sirens sang may not be beyond speculation, but the vagaries of English pronunciation? (Pedants will judge you remiss unless you say va.GARE.eez in reading the previous sentence.) I trust that you don't expect me to answer these questions.

Why matters less than _what_ in facing the name of the poet William Cowper and hearing the professor say without a smile that his name is pronounced K00.per. Consider an Anglo-American encounter once witnessed by Warren Fleischauer, former head of the English Department at Frostburg State: A short time after the end of World War II a troop train full of American soldiers pulled into an English town. A rough American, a nice mixture of the couth of Jethro Bodine, Judd Nelson, and Shelley Winters, boomed out to an English lad on the platform, "Say, what do you call this burg anyway?" The piping voice replied in English tones that wouldn't shimmy Jello, "We call it DAR.bee, Sir." He pointed to the sign "Derby," tacit criticism of the Yank's lack of observation hanging in the air. "Ha! back home we call that DER.bee. It sure looks like DER.bee to me." "You may call it what you will, Sir, but here we call it DAR.bee."

Who was right? I think I know what Miss Manners would say. Samuel Johnson said that we all have ourselves to cure of the desire to make people stare. Surely we must also cure ourselves of the desire to make others' ears flap? If Cowper said it was KOO.per (and he did), it is. If Derby says it's DAR.bee (and it does), it is. If the St. Johns stand still for being called SIN. jun (and they do), why jostle?

Probably the most mangled proper noun of all is Brontë, of Emily, Charlotte, Anne, and Branwell fame. Even the English, not usually Francophiles, want to turn this Irish name into Bron.TAY, as if the diaresis over the _e_ were just an affected way of achieving an acute accent, a _cafe_ type of word with pretensions. In English the diaresis over a vowel usually suggests that what your instinct would tell you to leave silent must be pronounced. The name as spelled in Ireland before the prodigies' father went over--Brunty— suggests a more reasonable, authentic pronunciation of Brontë--BRON.tee or BRUN.tee. Just try it and make people stare.

But the English, God bless 'em, won't be bossed around by anything so simpleminded as the equivalence of syllables and sounds to orthographic representation. The BBC has to instruct its English announcers how to pronounce English village names in the English fashion. Otherwise, some might not know that Ulgham spells UFF.am, Happisburgh spells HAZ. bruh, Hardenhuish is HARN.ish, Bagworthy is BAD.jer.ee, and --my favorite--Pucknowle is PUN.nel. Take that, you incorrigibly naive American, absorbing your sense of pronunciation from _spelling_, of all things.

Two Languages

[This piece was written as one of three parts of a collaboration on mathsemantics to be published in the journal ETC: A Review of General Semantics.]

A kind of tension, if not outright conflict, often exists between the languages of mathematics and ordinary English. Mathematics aims to say more with less than other languages--to be clear, precise, concise, logical. On the whole, it doesn't deal with fuzzy context. English, on the other hand, revels in, even wallows in, fuzzy context. It is logical when it is logical (and only then). Evolving usage and context--not careful definition as in math--determine what words mean.

Mathematics says more with less and yet expresses far fewer and far simpler, clearer concepts (no matter how abstruse the concepts) than ordinary English. Consider, for instance, the concept of the binomial theorem versus the concept of "justice." This paradox--that the language of mathematics is far simpler than ordinary English (tell that to the innumerate English major)--is one of those paradoxes that delight those who love both mathematics and English.

You would think that in a part of language so consciously and artificially constructed as numbers we would be free of paradox--that a number is abstracted from context and that *forty* can mean only "four tens." After all, mathematical language arises much later than most vernacular language, and the vernacular devises quantifiers--approximate quantities like *few*, *several*, and *many*--long before a system of exact numbers. So once a language has a word like *forty*, shouldn't the advantage of such precision over the muddy *many* be self-evident and eminently desirable?

Well, no: the vernacular often wants the indefinite and will perversely convey the indefinite by assigning to it a definite number value. *Forty* often means "relatively many," more than can be counted by a quick eyeballing.

This can easily be found in Hebraic, Greek, Persian, Roman, Arabic, and Turkish writers as well as in everyday English.

Thus, *The Arabian Nights* story of "Ali Baba and the Forty Thieves" suggests that there are a few dozen thieves, nothing so exact as twice twenty, storing their treasure in a cave. The Hebraic Bible, or Old Testament, has forty of almost everything of a sizable number, from days and nights of rain, to years of wandering in the wilderness, to the years reigned by both David and Solomon.

The slipperiness of *forty* as a number continues in our expression "forty winks," said of a short nap, especially after dinner; in "forty-'leven" to mean quite a few, as in "It stunk as bad as forty-'leven skunks"; in "forty miles from nowhere" to describe how far in the sticks one is; in "forty miles of bad road" for something or someone ineffably ugly; in "forty-gallon Baptist" to describe one zealous for total immersion; in "forty-legs" as a dialectical English (and Turkish and Persian!) name for the centipede; and in "forty acres" to describe unusually large feet, as in "The dance floor was quite crowded once he came in with his forty acres."

Perhaps no other number has the wonderful fuzziness, imprecision via a precise number, as *forty*. But all of you can probably furnish further examples. At first the ancient Greeks meant 10,000 by the number word *myriad*. It has been dozens of forty years, however, since anybody meant anything other than "a very large number" by speaking of a *myriad*.

And when the Italian says, "I'm going to take two steps about the garden before retiring," no one expects him to step outside and then step back in. Someone saying, "I can give you a half-dozen reasons" must not be faulted for not having exactly six.

What can be done about this sort of precise imprecision? Of course, nothing needs to be done to eliminate it, just to sensitize people to it. Every child needs to learn the conventions of language, and the different pull of mathematical language and the vernacular is one of those conventions. Every child, however, is a willful precisian, holding parents to the letter of what is said with a "But you said. . . ." A quite willful precisian indeed when I an importuning boy, I wanted to know just how long my mother's "just a moment" meant. I knew that "a" meant "one"; and, gullible little precisian that I was, I believed my brother's explanation that a moment is exactly ninety seconds, a minute and a half. Thus, I could gauge how long to wait before saying "But you said . . . ."

A more difficult matter is to acquaint oneself with cultural differences that make precise numbers just another aid to a rhetorical flourish, to the poetic metaphor that's not an untruth, just an emotive semantic signal, richly contextual. Probably not one person in ten who reads the Bible knows about the Semitic languages' use of *forty* as a rhetorical device. Probably no great harm is done by this ignorance. Still, we all know the harm that can be done by a credulous literalism in reading religious texts, as if writers never speak in metaphor. Teachers, not just of English but also of mathematics, among others, need to alert students to the precise and imprecise uses of numbers. They both have immense power.

The Greatness of Samuel Johnson

[This paper was presented at a monthly meeting of the Torch Club, where professionals speak about and discuss their intellectual interests, in Cumberland, Maryland, and was selected to be repeated at a large regional gathering of a number of local Torch Clubs in Hagerstown, Maryland.]

That Samuel Johnson lived to the age of 75 (1709-1784) is surprising. He wasn't expected to survive the first day. Born to a middle-aged mother, born almost dead, unable to cry for some time, he was baptized in his mother's bedroom the night of his birth, a sure sign that he was not expected to live. His Aunt Jane always said that she "would not have picked such a poor creature up in the street," so unlikely was he to survive and thrive. But he did. As a small child he survived scrofula--tuberculosis of the lymph glands--which left his face and neck scarred for life and later in life led to nervous tics and sudden starts and gesticulations, so that people sometimes took him for an inspired idiot. In childhood and much of his adult life he was blind in one eye; he was deaf in one ear. He was what can only be called constitutionally indolent, always of a mind to do just nothing--and then doing amazing amounts of work at breakneck speed. And he suffered from a morbid depression so intense that at times he himself said he would have been willing to cut off an arm or a leg if he thought it would recover his spirits.

The great raw-boned, prodigiously ugly young man went up to Oxford University only when he was 19, and left 13 months later. After this Johnson had no formal education; the doctorate is of course honorary. Early in his writing career he walked the streets of London all night or slept in the warm ashes of a glass factory because he had nowhere else to go. He got his name on the title page of a publication for the first time at age 40. Yet he succeeded so well that as we approached the end of the second millennium of the Christian era the *Washington Post* in a retrospective over the previous millennium named him "the smartest man" of the past

1,000 years and his *Dictionary of the English Language* as the greatest single book of those 1,000 years, "a triumph of a single human's will, and a lasting monument to learning and literacy." B. L. Reid, a fine critic and writer, erstwhile English professor at Mt. Holyoke College, says, "Johnson is the greatest of all Englishmen (by no means England's greatest writer) by virtue of massive powers of person and of personality . . . he is easy to attack and impossible to wound."

If this learned professor and these intelligent journalists heap such praise—the smartest man, the greatest book, the greatest Englishman--why do you hear so little about him and think so little about him? I thought a great deal about the man as I taught a course called "The Age of Johnson" roughly 20 times in my 30 years at Frostburg State University. I think that the *Washington Post* and B. L. Reid are right: this is an immeasurably great man--due more recognition than he gets.

Let us follow Boswell's implied main emphases in portraying the greatness of Samuel Johnson--the astonishing power of expression in impromptu conversation, the mental powers exhibited in his writing, and the magnificence of the man's moral nature.

Foremost in Boswell is Johnson talking, talking, talking. He was talking more than writing in the parts of a few hundred days that Boswell knew him in the last 20-some years of his life. According to Richard Altick, the recorded impromptus of all other human beings in history added together do not equal Johnson's in pleasure and value.

Altick adds that Johnson's capacities and complexities of personality thus revealed outstrip any fictional character's. Let's hear some impromptus on a miscellany of subjects:

Boswell and another man wrote a pamphlet attacking a weak play. Then the other man relented, saying that they had no right to abuse the tragedy, for neither he nor Boswell could write one nearly as good. Johnson: ". . . this is not just reasoning. You _may_ abuse a tragedy, though you cannot write one. You may scold a carpenter who has made you a bad table, though you cannot make a table."

Of James MacPherson, a writer who affected to be a savage and railed at all established systems: "He wants to make himself conspicuous. He would tumble in a hogstye, as long as you looked at him and called him to come out. But . . . never mind him, and he'll soon give it over."

In a group where a question had been asked about who a man was who left the gathering: "I do not care to speak ill of any man behind his back, but I believe the gentleman was an <u>attorney</u>."

The discussion being on politics and patriotism, Johnson vociferated, "Patriotism is the last refuge of a scoundrel"--and who, reading the letters to the editor of almost any small newspaper, can doubt it?

The difference between the English and the French: " . . . an Englishman is content to say nothing when he has nothing to say."

Of Bet Flint, a notorious woman of the town, who asked Johnson to write a preface to her autobiography in verse: "I used to say of her that she was generally slut and drunkard; occasionally, whore and thief."

Of a concerted effort to have fun: "Nothing is more hopeless than a scheme of merriment."

Last of the impromptus: In the eighteenth century it was the custom when meeting someone sailing or boating on the river Thames to accost the one met with abusive language. A boater thus attacked Johnson with coarse raillery, not recorded, and Johnson fired back, "Sir, your wife, under pretense of keeping a bawdy house, is a receiver of stolen goods." Let's unpack this wonderfully comic putdown, which most students hear without laughter. It says, "Your wife wants a cover to her illegal activity of being a fence, so she thinks of how to disguise her actions. Such is her moral poverty that the highest character she can imagine to cover her illicit activities is to be the madam of a whorehouse."

Closely allied to such powers of expression, of course, are the gigantic mental powers exhibited in his writing. Let's look at his three major works for evidence. The first in time and magnitude is the *Dictionary of the*

English Language of 1755, which the *Washington Post* called the greatest book of the second millennium of the Christian era. The foundation of all later English dictionaries, this massive work he did essentially by himself. When, more than a century later, the <u>New</u> English Dictionary (now the *Oxford English Dictionary*) was started, a much larger project eventually, ten times larger, it took 2300 scholars 71 years to complete. Johnson finished his in less than nine years and expected to do it in three. When Dr. William Adams told Johnson that it took the French Academy, composed of 40 men, 40 years to compile their dictionary, querying how he could expect to do it alone in three years, Johnson answered, "Let me see; forty times forty is sixteen hundred. As three to sixteen hundred, so is the proportion of an Englishman to a Frenchman." And nine to 1600 isn't a bad proportion either.

Consider the powers of mind required to be the first to write definitions of any substance for words like *come* and *go,* each subdivided into more than 50 submeanings, and 94 for *set,* which has the most numerous meanings in the *OED.* By common assent of the time, the English dictionary, written by one man, was better than the French and Italian dictionaries, written by whole academies of scholars.

Johnson's second large multi-yeared writing project was his edition of the works of Shakespeare, published in 1765. Of his work Walter Raleigh said in 1908 that "Johnson is able in one passage after another to go straight to Shakespeare's meaning, while the philological and antiquarian commentators kill one another in the dark." Johnson's reading of Shakespeare has been taken over and subsumed into the notes that help all readers' understanding of Shakespeare today. The *Variorum Shakespeare,* the 20th-century edition aiming at completeness of understanding of all that Shakespeare wrote, quotes Johnson on Shakespeare more than any other critic or editor--this though we have learned so much about the language in the past 240 years.

The third major work of Johnson's writing life was *The Lives of the Poets,* biographies ranging from a few pages to small books about 52 poets from the previous 100-plus years. Johnson preferred in biography the "minute details of daily life," thus giving to Boswell his chief method in portraying Johnson. Thus, we see the unforgettable portrait of Alexander Pope: ". . . when he had two guests in his house, he would set at supper a single pint [of wine] upon the table; and having himself taken two small glasses, would retire, and say, *Gentlemen, I leave you to your wine.*" A modern biographer of Pope has said that it is the best biography of Pope ever written. We also have the wonderful mix of judgment on a writer like John Milton. Of *Paradise Lost* Johnson said it is not the greatest epic only because it is not the *first*. Still, "None ever wished it longer." Any commentator on Milton to this day seems driven to begin with Johnson, trying to dispose of him. Every reader will sympathize with his judgment of the possibility of allegorical meaning in "Lycidas": the allegorical meaning is "so uncertain and remote" that it is "never sought because it cannot be known" when found.

Johnson himself would doubtlessly want to be most remembered for my last topic--his luminous moral nature. This man took his religion's injunction to be charitable quite literally, in every sense of the word. He supported and gave shares of his pension to a whole houseful of the world's castoffs--an uncouth doctor who worked in the worst slums of London and was rarely paid; a blind poetess who of course could not support herself; another woman, the daughter of the Lichfield doctor who betrayed Johnson's medical confidence when he was young; the black valet, whom Johnson did not need but whom Johnson had educated, rescued from a hard life at sea, and to whom Johnson left his estate. Finding a poor woman, a prostitute lying in the street, he took her on his back, paid for her care for a long period, and when her health was restored, exerted himself to get her into a virtuous way of living. He would empty his pockets of all of his silver to give to beggars, and when told on one occasion "He'll spend it on drink," Johnson responded, "And why *shouldn't* he?"

On a more abstract plane, he wrote the best, the only unanswerable criticism of the American Revolution: "How is it that we hear the loudest yelps for liberty among the drivers of negroes?" He always pungently attacked colonialism--in an age when all of the tide was running toward British colonialism and imperialism. He thought for himself, always.

He is also the author of perhaps the best moral-political dictum of all--"A decent provision for the poor is the true test of civilization"--a judgment that America would do well always to remember. He knows the "strength and sleepless craving of human egotism": "He who is growing great and happy by electrifying a bottle wonders how the world can be engaged by trifling prattle about war and peace." Or he speaks of the moralist "swelling with the [idea of] the applause which he will gain by proving that applause is of no value." This is a moralist generous in his comic understanding of our fractured ideals. I know of no other human being who can express so wittily and fully the complexities of how to be human, and that is always our hardest and most important how-to.

This is a great man, a compliment to human nature.

In Hemlock

[This was written after visiting one of the small but inspiring state parks in western Maryland.]

In hemlock woods the living clench the dead:
A sapling clings to moss, alive on stone;
Roots arch and splay, tips cascade and spread;
Then moss and stone, debris and mold, combine,

Giving life to rocky slope. Here and there,
In jackstrawed tumble the deadfalls lie,
Year by year declining to what they were,
As seedlings root at head and foot, wet and dry.

In standing snag, beneath the bark, is life--
Insects, bats, and birds that breed and grow;
On standing snag, for lookout perch, alight
Osprey and hawk; here live bobcats and bear.

All concatenate, linking life and death:
Leaves fall to forest floor, lichens rain to earth,
Fungus spawns on logs, truffles underneath;
The wood secures itself as death gives birth.

Some Oddities of the English Language:
How They Came About

[This paper was also written for oral presentation at a Torch Club meeting.]

If we consider the numbers of native speakers of the several thousand languages of the world, English clearly does not rank first. Mandarin Chinese, with well over 800 million native speakers, claims that distinction. Still, Mandarin, spoken only in the northern regions of China and in Singapore, has little world-wide influence compared to English, and almost nobody has Mandarin as the chosen second language. English is clearly the second language of choice for most of the world, and the number of people who can speak a good deal of English ranges somewhere between 750 million and one billion. English is more nearly universal than any other language has ever been. That not-the-first language of a tiny island--Albion--has become so dominant is a striking story in itself. And though all languages are idiosyncratic, English is surely among the most idiosyncratic of all, presenting both special challenges and special ease for those who would learn the language.

In some respects English is one of the most difficult of languages; in other respects, it is among the simplest. Both the difficulties and the simplicities are rooted inextricably in the language's history. We probably cannot get rid of the difficulties, and we do not want to get rid of the simplicities. The difficulties we owe primarily to literacy and learning and the archconservatism that follows. The simplicities we owe mostly to invasion, illiteracy, and loss.

Perhaps the greatest difficulty to non-native speakers of English— and to most native speakers--is the strange mismatch of spelling and pronunciation. We are certainly not the only language to have inconsistent spelling. French is consistently inconsistent, with the -ue of words ending in -gue being silent and the -s at the ends of words not being pronounced unless a vowel follows. Irish is inconsistently consistent. How, for instance, would you spell the Irish girl's name [neeve]? Surely the usual spelling,

Niamh, is counter-intuitive. Still, it's mostly a matter of learning that the -v- sound is spelled -mh-, unless it's spelled -bh- or -bhf. English, on the other hand, is inconsistently inconsistent. Have you heard the linguist's favorite nonsense riddle: How does one spell fish in English? The answer is *ghoti*, the -gh- spelling /f/ as in *rough*; the -o- spelling /i/ as in *women*; the -ti- spelling /sh/ as in *nation*. Ghoti, /f/, /i/, /sh/ = fish. Of course, this is nonsense, as I hope George Bernard Shaw knew. The -gh- never spells /f/ at the beginning of words, -ti- never spells /sh/ at the end of words, and -o- spells /i/ in only one word in English.

President Andrew Jackson purportedly said, "It's a damn' poor mind can think of only one way to spell a word." English is perhaps the only language in which the spelling bee is practiced, to teach children the one way to spell a word. At the root of the problem is the disjunction between the Germanic language English and the Roman alphabet adopted to write English upon the Christianization of the English beginning in the late 6th century. English has around 43 or 44 distinct sounds, or phonemes. The Roman alphabet, if we adhere to the ideal--that each letter should spell one sound and one sound only--can spell only 23 sounds. (We have to toss out c or k, q, and x.) No totally new or retained graphemes have been added to English since the 6th century. And English, quite differently from many European languages stuck with an inadequate alphabet, has never added diacritics, like, say, Spanish or Swedish. So spelling and pronunciation are going to be difficult from the outset.

Add to this inrooted problem the Norman French conquest of 1066. French was to be the dominant language of literature, the law, government, and all dominion for the next few hundred years. Norman scribes did most of the writing, even of English texts, sometimes not knowing English very well, certainly not pronouncing it well, importing French irrationalities for Old English spellings that made more sense. For instance, an Old English word was spelled *cniht* (knight), and every letter was pronounced consistently, approximately /kanicht/. Norman scribes spelled the /h/ sound -gh- in England, and the Middle English spelling of the word is usually *knyght*, the -gh- sound not easily pronounced by the French tung (which the Norman scribes spelled *tongue*); nor could the French easily pronounce a /k/ sound followed by an /n/ sound.

When printing is introduced to England, in 1476, the first printers are from the continent, with continental languages, habits, and biases, just at the time that English is undergoing its primary change in pronunciation of all time--the Great Vowel Shift. For instance, consider the /i/ sound in *time* versus the continental /i/ sound of *machine*; or the /e/ sound of *the* versus the /e/ sound of *cafe*. These printers of course needed to regularize spelling for type-setting. Thus, the sounds of the main vowels are just in the process of changing from the continental values just as printers are freezing the continental spellings. There's little chance of retreating or ever solving these spelling and pronunciation oddities satisfactorily.

A second great oddity of English is the bewildering richness of its vocabulary. We have by far the largest vocabulary of any of the world's languages--at least two to three times as many words as whatever is in second place (Russian?). Frequently our history has left us with triads of words: the Anglo-Saxon *ask*; the Norman French *question*; the learned Latin *interrogate*. Only a tone-deaf person would say that the three mean exactly the same. We need all three--and dozens of other verbs to cover the same general area of meaning. Sir Walter Scott pointed out that we have the conquered English for *pig, cow, calf,* and *sheep*; the conqueror French for *pork, beef, veal,* and *mutton*. We clearly do not praise the "roast cow of old England." We need all eight words. And we raid nearly every language of the world for vocabulary, Englishing them willy-nilly. From Hebrew we have *jubilee*; from Italian *fiasco*; from Persian via Hindi *khaki*; from Chinese via Malay *ketchup*; from Arabic *alcohol*; from Kimbundu, a Bantu language, *banjo*, etc., etc., times tens of thousands.

What is the speaker of English to do with a vocabulary of at least half a million words? Few of us can master more than a small fraction of our language's wordhoard. The joy is in the chase. And two Williams, Shakespeare and Faulkner--using a larger portion of their language than even most writers--found a fraction of the immense vocabulary adequate and more.

Consider the last great difference we will look at: Our grammar is very simple. Before you ask "What?!" in astonishment, I repeat, "Our grammar is very simple." I am using *grammar* in the true sense, how a language communicates meaning, not to mean *usage*. Consider, for instance, how a great many European languages deal with gender. To learn German you need to know that *girl* is neuter, *das Mädchen* (with an umlaut over the *-a-*); that *question* is feminine, *die Frage*; and that *head cold* is masculi*ne, der Schnupfen*. English, at root a Germanic language, used to be the same. No more: *the* girl; *the* question, *the* head cold. Nor do we have to change the article to agree with the number of the noun. We say "the girls," as opposed to, say, "die Mädchen." When the case changes--when the noun changes from subject of the sentence to a direct object, for instance--German has to say *den Schnupfen*. In English we say "The girl hit the ball" or "The ball hit the girl." Old English had inflections, especially on the ends of word roots, such as *nama* for subject, *naman* for direct object, *namena* for plural possessive, and *namum* for plural object of SOME prepositions. But these inflections being in an unstressed syllable led to all of the vowels becoming a schwa (the sound of the first -e- in *antelope*), whether spelled with an a, e, i, o, u, or y. So English inflections, never nearly so numerous as in Greek and Latin, simplified further in order to communicate with the Northmen who conquered much of England in the 9th and 10th centuries, Old Norse being similar enough to English except in the inflectional endings. To adapt large numbers of French words, with yet another inflectional system, to English, speakers communicated mostly by dropping inflections. English had always had a strong tendency to communicate meaning by where the word was in the sentence. Heavily inflected languages have difficulty borrowing foreign words, but a lightly inflected English, with a very wide variety of sounds, in addition to syllable structure and stress, made borrowing easy.

All of which leads us to the great and wonderful simplicity of English grammar, except in pronouns and a few other things. English communicates meaning in the sentence primarily by where the word is. Thus we can take a noun, *road*, precede it with another noun, *rail*, then put them both in front of another noun, *car*, and the first two nouns become an adjective, *railroad* car. We can say "railroad car design" or even "railroad car design competition" with perfect clarity and brevity. This simple beauty--that any part of speech can become other parts of speech--makes English flexible and easy to shape into meaning. The child says "But . . .," and the mother responds "But me no buts," turning a conjunction into an imperative verb and a count noun in the space of four words. The child says, *"I think it's pretty!"* The mother responds, "If you don't get that off your face right now, I'll pretty you." Now an adjective is a verb. Or Shakespeare can say in a sonnet "And yet, by heaven, I think my love as rare/ As any she belied by false compare," where *she*, ordinarily a pronoun, is here a noun, meaning "woman," and *compare*, ordinarily a verb, is here a noun. Ain't English grand?

Loutish Gardener to Sensitive Plant

[I wrote this in response to an interviewer who assumed that I love gardening for the same reason she does—to rescue stressed plants.]

You, finicky plant, tell me why,

When all about you *want* to live,

And will, given half a chance,

You must sulk and sull, pule and pine.

Why should I coddle you and strive

To prop your head, fainting and limp,

When thousands of plants pulse with life?

If pine you must--die, damn you, die.

Words as Images and Figures

[This paper is a short extract from one of the chapters of *Word Study*, which I wrote to use as a text in my course of the same name at Frostburg State University.]

Images that appeal to the senses, especially sight, vivify everyday language, making it more expressive. Some of the most vivid images are figures of speech, not used merely to decorate but to explain. The poet, of course, is expected to be metaphorical--to compare lovers to roses, Assyrians to wolves, or evenings to etherized patients. Yet everyone has some natural inclination to metaphor, if only in common expressions and cliches such as "It's raining cats and dogs. (I know because I see rain poodles all over.)" This tendency of language to be figurative is a boon to the dedicated word-hoarder, for a figure, by its nature, summons a concrete image to explain an abstract idea. Despite our being educated more and more in abstract thought as we get older, we live primarily in our sense impressions. Once we deposit a sense impression in our memory bank, a previously abstract word is more easily remembered, to be withdrawn on demand.

For instance, consider the word *kowtow*, a word of figurative etymology, from the Chinese. It literally means "to knock head," used of the deferential act of the Chinese, bowing in respect or submission, touching the ground with their heads. Once this literal picture is imagined, it is easy to comprehend the figurative idea, the general concept: to kowtow is to pay homage to, to defer to, even to be obsequiously attentive to someone or something. We can say, "I'm not going to kowtow to his opinions just because he's my boss; he is certainly wrong this time." Or the mother who expects her daughter to pay scrupulous attention to what the neighbors might think may be rebuffed with "Why should I kowtow to public opinion of the primmest kind?"

Panache further illustrates the aid of figurative etymology in strengthening vocabulary. The word comes from an Old French term meaning "tuft or plume of feathers" such as worn on a helmet. A plume of feathers on a helmet has no absolute military service, but the flamboyance of style, the dash and elegance of appearance, no doubt served as a psychological boost to the warrior. Anyone with this flamboyance, this dash, is said to have panache. A football player might run down the field with panache; an actor might exhibit panache in the smallest role and steal a scene from more sedate actors.

One last example for now: *Supercilious* is a favorite example, if for no other reason than that it sounds too extravagantly figurative to be credited. *Super* is from the Latin for "above," and the other part of the word is known to biology students who have seen a paramecium under a microscope. The waving hairlike fringe around the microbe is called *cilia,* the Latin for "eyelid" or "eyelashes." Consider the scientist's plight: Adam-like, he or she has to name previously unobserved phenomena. The scientist would no doubt feel silly calling microbial hair-like appendages "eyelashes," but saying the same thing in Latin or Greek attains the learned tone and universality at the same time. The one-step-removed figure obscures the image for the uninitiated; but once you see the figure, *cilia* is unforgettable. *Supercilium*, then, is Latin for "eyebrow" ("above the eyelid"). The raised brows of hauteur account for this quaint connection of a concrete facial part and an abstract emotion. *Supercilious* means "arrogant, disdainful, haughtily contemptuous." A supercilious person arches the eyebrow, looks down the nose, and withers another person with disdain. Combining two favorite images of P. G. Wodehouse, we may say that a supercilious person looks like a duchess eyeing a caterpillar in the bottom of a salad bowl.

The Word and the Number

[This paper was presented as introductory material at a math symposium at Frostburg State University.]

So what's a professor of English--even a retired one--doing at a math symposium? As an undergraduate, I would not have found it strange, for I was a double major--in mathematics first and then in English, having the bare minimum of credit hours in English and half again as many hours in math. When I chose to go to graduate school in English and to become a college English professor, of course I forgot most of the math above the level of college algebra and found myself channeled into ever more specialized academic areas, putting the two together only rarely, as in reading the literature of that great mathematician Lewis Carroll. However, ask me anything you want about what Samuel Johnson said about almost anything. I don't think that he ever said anything about mathsemantics. Still, he did say, ". . . the good of counting [is that] it brings every thing to a certainty which before floated in the mind indefinitely."

Our society at the very beginning of the twenty-first century does a great deal more counting than England did in the late eighteenth century. Yet the counting often doesn't bring anything to a certainty; indeed, it often makes matters float *more* indefinitely in the mind. For instance, apparently the majority of the people in the world think that it takes only ninety-nine years to make up the century that we called the twentieth.

Our English students usually don't want to count anything: they throw up their hands and surrender in the first skirmish with a word problem in math. Our math students often don't want to fret about what ambiguity *means*: they smile sardonically at English students' finding meaning in some puzzling lyric poem by, say, Gerard Manley Hopkins. Neither group listens sympathetically to my insistence that both the math problem and the English poem call upon the same abilities, requiring understanding of how language works. They don't understand that a whole person cannot divorce mathematics from larger language concerns.

Both groups, for example, are almost certain to give erroneous answers to the question of how old the speaker is in A. E. Housman's poem "Loveliest of Trees":

> Now, of my threescore years and ten,
> Twenty will not come again.

Now this is as unambiguous as can very well be, a mildly poetic statement of the obvious--the speaker is twenty years old, expecting a life span of fifty more years. But at least 80% of my students fumble the answer, even when Housman says it twice more in the poem:

> And take from seventy springs a score,
> It only leaves me fifty more.

> And since to look at things in bloom
> Fifty springs are little room . . . .

If it were only an occasional lyric poem that led to confusion in expressing or understanding numerical ideas, the world might very well wag on much as it has. However, we need cooperation between number people and word people because nearly all of us today are, perforce, both: we use numbers and have to communicate those numbers to others in unambiguous words. One of my near-despairs as a composition instructor was how unclear students can be in presenting evidence in support of a thesis-- paradoxically both suspicious of numbers, not wanting to use them, and blatantly unskeptical about printed numbers, statistics, percentages that are patently absurd.

What we call "illegitimate additions" or "displaced counts" especially interest me. A former president of Frostburg State, in competition with Towson State for Maryland funding, voiced his suspicion that Towson, to determine its number of students, counted every student in a car that drove through the campus as a student each time the student drove through.

Thus, if this suspicion were just, Towson would get an illegitimate count of students and greater funding, perhaps for more students than the campus facilities would hold. Doubtless you could add to the anecdotal store of how illegitimate counts affect education and funding and some aspect of your working life.

This is part of why I'm here--to examine how language works in giving us squirrely numbers.

How Much Littler? How Much Bigger?

[Again, I am dealing with the differences between the two major languages that we use here, English and mathematics, part of a large colloquium on mathsemantics.]

If English inadequately or ambiguously expresses numerical comparisons, the reasons are complex, grammatical, and historically deep-rooted. Seeking and finding cures will not be easy.

At the root of the problem is how English compares anything. Originally, adjectives were only inflected, nearly all adjectives adding what became -*er* for a higher degree and -*est* for the highest degree among the qualities compared. Note that English used and still uses no inflection for the same degree and had and has no inflection for a lower degree.

A second way to compare qualities gained ground under French influence after the Norman Conquest: a syntactic or periphrastic way of expressing degree--*more* or *most* + the adjective for a higher degree and *less* or *least* + the adjective for a lower degree. We routinely use this kind of comparison for longer adjectives such as *beautiful*. A great many of this kind of comparison for longer adjectives came into English from Norman French (after 1066), and it is difficult to say "beautifuller." But to use *less* or *least*, we have to say something like "less large" when we want to say something like "smaller."

Thus, any quality that might be construed as a "minus comparison" involves a paradox: We can speak only of a *higher* degree of a *lower* quality, so to speak, such as *smaller* or *shorter* for a *higher* degree of something *less*. Or we can say that something is "less big" when we want to say "smaller." Linguistically, it is but a short leap to saying something like "three times smaller" and thus to flip-flop multiplication and division. Our language almost makes us do it, though many people cringe upon hearing a term of multiplication used for its inversion. They need not.

Use of the word *times* for multiplication--with us since at least the late fourteenth century (*OED*)--resulted in at least two meanings in mathematical contexts. The first is that the clear noun/substantive *time* can simply mean "an instance of," as in "She has been married three times." Given that the historical idiom for "thrice as often" is "three times more than," the muddy writer will say something as vague as "She has been married three times more than I have," and we don't know whether to add or do complex addition--multiplication. The second meaning that complicates matters is the use of *times* for division as well as multiplication. This meaning is so deep-rooted linguistically that it is a much more difficult matter to disentangle. Editorial intervention will not be enough.

Indeed, dictionaries today, post-1961, when Merriam-Webster's *Third New International* unabridged was published, more and more just describe educated usage and do not *prescribe* what someone may think *ought* to be done-- description rather than prescription. Thus, *The American Heritage Dictionary of the English Language,* the edition of 2000, says of *times,* "Used to indicate the number of instances by which something is multiplied or divided. *This tree is three times taller than that one. My library is many times smaller than hers.* Other excellent American dictionaries essentially agree: *times* indicates the number of instances by which something is divided as well as multiplied. *Webster's Third New International* gives this as the second definition of *times:* "equal fractional parts of which an indicated number equal a comparatively greater quantity <seven times smaller> <three times closer>."

The ordinary speaker or writer little cares that *times* is from the Indo-European root meaning "to divide." As Schwartzman says, "When we say 'five times three,' we are saying that a larger amount, in this case fifteen, can be divided into five groups of three . . . . In English, the meaning of *time* shifted from the divisional to the multiplicative aspect of the operation."

That common usage would hold on to the etymological sense of the word *times* owes nothing to a fondness for etymology; rather it seems to be an aversion to fractions and to losing one's desired word of emphasis. Thus, rather than say "one-third as large," most people prefer saying "three times smaller."

Fear of fractions is endemic, even, it appears, among intelligent people. For instance, my high school algebra teacher talked a student into adding algebra to his schedule, knowing that he had the abstract reasoning necessary for that higher-than-required mathematics course. The student dropped out of the course on the second day, saying, "I didn't know that it dealt with fractions." Just so, we would rather invert the mathematical process and not call upon the antithetical adjective--not "one-tenth as far" but "ten times closer."

Does saying something like "three times more" introduce ambiguity? Not historically, but we do not live in the linguistic past, though tied to it. Usage is usually slow to change. *More* is doing double duty, both the *more* used for the comparative and *more* in the sense of "something additional" that seems to invoke the idea of adding to a base. We need to examine more closely how English uses comparisons of varying degrees.

To express the *same* degree of a quality, English has never had an inflectional ending, relying instead on the syntactic or periphrastic construct *as. . . as* (in Old English *swa . . . swa*)--for example "You have just *as* many *as* I do"--the comparison of equals.

In order to speak of a comparatively superior or inferior degree of some quality, the grammar of English required--and some would say still requires--a construction with *than*. Perhaps the all-time foremost authority on the grammar of English, Otto Jespersen, said, in 1958, that superiority and inferiority, any *in*equality of comparison, requires *than*. This leads us to expressions like "The number is three times larger than expected." Quirk, Greenbaum, et al., later supreme experts on English, say that comparisons in English require a correlative construction--*more* or *less* correlating with *than* and, for equals, *as* correlating with *as*.

A more recent grammarian, of apparently transformational bent, expresses the same idea in a book with the astonishing title *A Grammar of English on Mathematical Principles*: " . . . when the comparative quantity is specified, *more than* loses its meaning contribution to the sentence and becomes a synonym for *as . . . as.*"

In the past, one could not grammatically use *as . . . as* for an *in*equality. One could not say "three times *as large as*" or "three times *as many as,*" for the expressions did not make grammatical sense. The expressions would have been "three times *larger than*" or "three times *more than.*" Nor could anyone upon hearing the expressions misconstrue them as meaning "as large as and then add a three-multiple" to get four times the original size. We have reams of evidence that in the era of human discourse when percentages were rarely used no ambiguity was created by either "three times larger than" or "three times smaller than." The expressions were idiomatic, and idioms do not require logic.

Now, however, we use percentages constantly, such expressions as "37% more" and "300% larger than." Percentages confuse the matter because the same wording will not work. "300% larger than" does *not* give thrice the smaller. Importing, by analogy, the language of percentages to simple multiples creates ambiguity and confusion. No one can say that ambiguity and confusion are good when numbers are involved.

How do we deal with ambiguity and confusion? The French have *l'Academie francaise* to try to dictate what must be done for the good of the language. The English, and English-speaking peoples everywhere, have always rejected the idea of a language academy. Samuel Johnson said, " . . . I, who can never wish to see dependence multiplied, hope the spirit of English liberty will hinder or destroy [any plan for an English language academy]." This from the foremost lexicographer and regularizer of the tongue through the eighteenth century.

Failing the establishment of an Academy, usage becomes the concern of "teachers, publishers, and self-appointed usage guardians." The "scholarly concept of usage as a social consensus based on the practices of the educated middle class" has been the development of only the past 100 years. Guides to usage contradict each other, perhaps guided by more concern or less concern for mathematical uses, perhaps some guided more by the desire for description rather than prescription. The best usage in mathematical language is that which conveys clear meaning, retaining all necessary distinctions.

Such usage need not be clearly logical, for language moves under many more dictates than logic. Who can explain the logic of most idioms? Intellectual argument, however, comes not amiss. Linguistic matters most easily influenced by intellectual argument are doubtlessly social or moral concerns such as gender equality and the value of non-prejudicial language. We have seen a revolution in these two areas in the last forty years.

Intellectual argument can be brought to bear on mathematical language, especially if it can be shown that confusion in mathematics is against one's self-interest and *is* a social concern.

"He's So Tight He Would Geld a Louse and Send the Testicles to Market"

[This examination of miserliness was written for "Grammarphone," a recurring column in the *Times-News*, a newspaper in Cumberland, Maryland.]

When I regularly volunteered to answer our Grammarphone, a writer's hotline at Frostburg State University, where I taught, we would frequently get questions about the intricacies of word meaning and etymology. One such question is "Is *niggardly*, meaning stingy, a racist word in its origin?"

No, it isn't. Despite being unfortunately similar in sound to the base epithet *nigger*, the noun *niggard* has nothing to do with racial bigotry. Indeed, this word for a stingy person is 400 years older than the racial slur. Geoffrey Chaucer, writing in the late fourteenth century, used *niggard* quite often, as did his contemporary John Wyclif. The word seems to derive from Scandinavia as there are similar forms in Old Norse and Norwegian.

Our language shows that though we consider saving money to be a virtue, we honor the golden mean here as elsewhere and hold extreme closeness to be mean-spirited, contemptible, and sometimes comic. A modern American is more likely to use *penny-pincher* or *tightwad* than *niggard*. *Tightwad* originated in America, where the miser had more than pennies to pinch--a whole wad, or roll of paper money, to hold tight. The phrase *penny peeler* is sometimes used in British English, but *tightwad* was imported by the British in the 1930s.

British thieves' slang from around 1700 gives us the satisfying sneer-word *skinflint*. Any word that has internal rhyme, that opens with a snap of the teeth, is a masterpiece of sarcasm. The idea of stinginess is vividly conveyed: a skinflint is so stingy he would skin a flint to save or gain something.

The most common word for a stingy person is *miser,* though 200 years younger in English than *niggard. Miser* is from the Latin for "wretched" and still carries the suggestion of greater meanness of living than the other words. The same Latin source-word gives us *misery* and *miserable,* both via French. The different suggestions or connotations of near-synonyms are often due to the origin of the words. Thus, a miser is not just stingy but comfortless and wretched, pinched in by his stinginess.

And of course when one wants to be very precise and memorable, one can draw on not just a single word and its etymological richness but on the strengths of figurative language, as the Irish hyperbole of this article's title does.

Unexpected Origins of Some Common Expressions

[This little piece was written for publication in the recurring newspaper column "Grammarphone."]

Let's look at some common expressions that everyone knows: *down in the dumps, flash in the pan, brand-new,* and *apple-pie order.* This seeming miscellany is linked together by a shared factor--each phrase contains a common word whose most common meaning apparently has no connection with the origin of the phrase. That is, *down in the dumps* has nothing to do with refuse heaps; *flash in the pan* nothing to do with the kitchen; *brand-new* nothing to do with name brands; and *apple-pie order* perhaps nothing to do with apples, alas. Where can one find certitude?

Mere perverseness is not what explains these curiosities of language. Rather, they rest on the rock of tradition--where our language has been, how it has had to work, how it changes.

Down in the dumps, meaning "in low spirits," dates from at least the early 1500s and was already much used by Shakespeare's day. *Dump* for a pile of refuse is primarily American, a rather new use, only about a century old. The 1500s used *dump* as a name for a sad tune or song. The word in this sense and in the meaning of dejection seems to come for the Dutch *domp,* dullness or mental haze.

A flash in the pan is an effort or a person that doesn't live up to early promise: short-lived brilliance. (I remember my Uncle Ernest shortsightedly predicting that Willie Mays would be just a flash in the pan. But he was a fan of the Yankees.) *Flash in the pan* comes from musketry: the flintlock rifle of the 1600s would not fire if the priming powder burned quickly in the "pan" of the gun and did not ignite the main charge.

To say something is *brand-new* seems a needless insistence. How much newer than new is brand-new? Absolutely unused. The degree of newness is defined by the phrase's origin in blacksmithing. A brand-new item was newly wrought, straight from the smithy's fire, or brand. French and German have equivalent forms--*funkelnagelneu* and *tout battant neuf*-- and Shakespeare used *fire-new*. *Brand*--meaning fire, flame, or a piece of burning wood--is as old as English itself, part of the Germanic word-stock carried to Britannia.

Last, and most problematic, *apple-pie order*. Many dictionaries that define this term for precise neatness do not venture a speculation about its origin. (Etymology is often part detection, part luck in reading, part educated guesswork, part foolhardiness.) The earliest citation of the phrase in written literature dates from 1780. Oddly, several early citations show the phrase used by shipmen. All guesses about the ranging of ingredients to make apple pies, the stacking of pies in New England cupboards, the chanting of "A is for apple pie" in alphabet books are merely surmise, documented with no hard written evidence.

The most learned guesses to date: (1) *cap-a-pie*, the English form of the French "head to foot" that is used in *Hamlet*. Give a bold, bald English pronunciation, and "cap-a-pie order" can slide into "apple-pie order" and make sense too. (2) *nappes-pliees*, the French for "folded linen." "Folded-linen order" makes sense, but the phrase could become "apple-pie order" only to the eye, not the ear. And the phrase cannot be documented by written evidence any more than the others. The only honest conclusion is that, so far, nobody knows. Maybe apples do indeed have something to do with the phrase after all.

Not Room To Swing a Cat

[This article was adapted from one written for the newspaper column "Grammarphone."]

When people complain that there isn't room to swing a cat, are they to be dismissed as grumps with unreasonable demands? How much room does it take to swing a cat anyway? A less grotesque image but perhaps just as forceful is the time-honored description of the drunk as "three sheets to [or in] the wind." What does a sot have to do with washday? Other common expressions evoke strange images: a servile person, a yes-man, is said to be toadying; someone who admits an error is said to be eating humble pie; and someone who talks arrant nonsense is accused of spouting claptrap, a satisfyingly contemptuous dismissal that sounds just right.

Quite clearly, sense images--primarily pictures--play a big part in expressive everyday language. The poet, of course, is expected to be metaphorical--to compare lovers to roses, Assyrians to wolves, or evenings to etherized patients. Yet everyone has some natural inclination to metaphor, if only in common expressions and cliches. It is a limp expression to say "It's 96 degrees and very humid," but quite a different matter to say "It's as hot as the hinges on the trapdoor of hell."

Common expressions revel in images. To study the etymology of some of the expressions--the origin and history of meaning--may dispel the vivid picture of a tabby cat twirled around someone's head to measure room-size, but there will be a clear gain in understanding the idea of the expression. Still, images remain.

"Claptrap" is a theatrical term: an actor would give a showy performance to trap claps, applause, no matter how empty of real drama the performance was. Today, the word signifies empty, showy, and cheap nonsense.

Since the person who eats humble pie has been humbled, we think that we know the origin of that phrase. But the genuine etymology is revealing. The original phrase was "umble pie," identical in sound to "humble pie" in most pronunciations. The umbles--dear innards and entrails--were given to social underlings following a medieval deer-hunt. The aristocrats dined on venison, the houndsmen on umbles. To eat humble pie is to abase oneself.

A toady was originally a toad-eater, the stooge who helped a medicine man sell his cure-alls by eating or pretending to eat the so-called poisonous toad, only to be miraculously cured by the snake-oil the mountebank was selling.

In old sailing language a "sheet" is the line attached to a sail that controls the set of the sail. If all three sheets are slackened, or "in the wind," the sails ran free, without control; and the ship was like a staggering drunk.

And, last, "room to swing a cat." The cat appears to be a cat-o'-nine-tails, the whip used to flog sailors. The earliest recorded use of the phrase is by Tobias Smollett, himself an old tar turned novelist, to whom calling the whip a cat was as natural as to grouse and grumble. (Laurence Sterne gave him the nickname Smelfungus.)

Not Very Like a Whale

[Written for *Gramma*.]

"I'm so hungry I could eat the south end of a northbound skunk."

"He's so tight he'd geld a louse and send the testicles to market."

"The floor of this bar is as slick as deer guts on a doorknob."

Indelicate remarks, these--but full of rude vigor. The blunt force suggests that the speakers are rural, older folk. Not just everybody knows what "to geld" means (though the context makes it clear). Not just everyone has had dealings with deer guts, on doorknobs or elsewhere. True, the second simile quoted above is a folk expression, origin unknown. But I know where I got the first and third--from college composition students under twenty--and they both borrowed them from home. The young woman who penned the first figure said, "That's what my father always says." The young man who applied his remark to a redneck bar said he had often heard the deer guts image.

"I hope it is no very cynical asperity," as Samuel Johnson would say in an altogether different register, to fear that our language is losing such poetic pith. I don't say bring back the blood and guts: we *are* more squeamish than the past in some respects. But I do say let's have a bit more sinew and muscle.

The vitality of language often lies in figurative language. Almost every speaker is drawn to similes to express HOW black something is, HOW blind someone is, HOW hot something is, using the standard "AS . . . . AS" construction for the simile, the figurative comparison.

Unfortunately, the comparisons that work are taken up so often that they become cliches. Once a speaker unthinkingly plugs in a tired comparison, we lose all pith and vigor, and even sense. "As clear as a bell" makes sense, tired as it is, when we are talking about clear sound. But one hears statements like this: "Now that I've cleaned up the underbrush, the path is as clear as a bell." Huh? Or one will hear from a babysitter answering a query about how the children behaved, "They were as good as gold." In payment of a debt, the children would work as well as gold? Holy gibberish, Batman!

Sometimes all a simile needs to regain freshness is for the speaker to extend and elaborate and literalize the cliche--not "as hot as hell" but "It's as hot as the hinges on the trapdoor of hell."

The composer of thousands of memorable similes and other comparisons of the figurative kind, with not just vivid but wildly comic comparisons, is P. G. Wodehouse. Let's see how he does it. "Aunt Dahlia was staring at Jeeves like a bear about to receive a bun." "When Lord Ickenham began to express and fulfil himself, strong men quivered like tuning forks." "Even at normal times Aunt Dahlia's map tended a little towards the crushed strawberry. But never had I seen it take on so pronounced a richness as now. She looked like a tomato struggling for self-expression." "He was as meek and mild a young man as you could meet in a day's journey. He had flaxen hair, weak blue eyes and the general demeanour of a saintly but timid cod-fish." "I don't suppose he makes enough out of a novel to keep a midget in doughnuts for a week. Not a really healthy midget." "You couldn't place it exactly because it was so long since you had read the book, but he reminded you of something out of *Pilgrim's Progress*." "Something that Edgar Allan Poe might have written on a rainy Sunday." "Warm though the morning was, he shivered, as only a confirmed bachelor gazing into the naked face of matrimony can shiver." "Jeeves lugged my purple socks out of the drawer as if he were a vegetarian fishing a caterpillar out of his salad." "Jeeves let his brain out another notch." "It was a poetic drama, and the audience, though loath to do anybody an injustice, was beginning to suspect that it was written in blank verse." "He would walk ten miles in the snow to chisel a starving orphan out of tuppence." "As a sleuth you are poor. You couldn't detect a bass drum in a telephone booth." "If I saw him perishing with thirst, I wouldn't give him the dew off a Brussels-sprout."

"He gave the book a tentative prod with the tip of his fingers, like a puppy pawing at a tortoise."

Good comparisons are fresh, imagistic, often with an elongated set of details that the reader or listener can imagine but has not heard before and would not have thought of: a bear about to get a sweet roll; how tuning forks vibrate; a bass drum in a telephone booth; how a puppy investigates a tortoise.

The Comedy of P. G. Wodehouse

[This appreciation was written specifically for my blog *Words, Words, Words*.]

Of all the writers I have read in English, the most constantly funny one is Pelham Grenville Wodehouse. Known to his friends as "Plum" (Say his first name fast, in your plummiest English accent), this man, his last name pronounced "Woodhouse," could make a cat laugh, if the cat could read.

As a young man, he spent a couple of years working in a bank, bored to his eyeballs, but soon was able to make a living writing for boys' magazines and humor periodicals, never looking back. He published just about 100 full-length fictions (I have all but one of them, a piece of juvenilia). Interspersed with these and some drama, his works often came out of America (He had dual citizenships), writing lyrics for musical comedies with the likes of Guy Bolton and Jerome Kern. He once had five musicals running simultaneously on Broadway. He also did a stint in Hollywood.

Living into his 94th year, knighted 45 days before he died, Wodehouse created multi-book series around some of his finest creations: Mr. Mulliner, the Scheherazade of the Angler's Rest Pub, holding forth about many of his relations and acquaintances; Uncle Fred; grifters like Stanley Featherstonehaugh Ukridge (pronounced YEWK.ridg); Psmith (the p is silent), a favorite individual character of mine; his most famous of all, Bertie Wooster and Jeeves; and, if possible, topping even this pair, my all-time favorite, Clarence, the 9th Earl of Emsworth and the Blandings Castle denizens, not the least of which is the Empress of Blandings, Clarence's pig, always in danger of being nobbled. The Empress has top-medaled several years running in the Fat Pigs category of Shropshire's agricultural fairs.

Here is God's plenty in major and minor characters: Bertie, of very little brain; Jeeves, his gentleman's gentleman, commenting by clearing his throat like some sheep on a distant hillside; Bertie's aunts--Agatha, who, according to Bertie, commits child sacrifice by moonlight and wears barbed wire next to her skin, and Dahlia (pronounced DAY.lee.a), red-faced and robust from years of view-hallooing after the foxes of old England; Clarence, the fuzz-brained earl who can never find his shirt studs to dress for dinner and uses paper clasps instead; his brother, Galahad Threepwood, ever swilling down cocktails mixed by the butler, Beach; and their sister Connie, as redoubtable as sisters and aunts always are who have to deal with feckless men; Sir Gregory Parsloe-Parsloe, a baronet neighbor of Clarence, rival in pig raising, and one knows what evil lurks in the hearts of baronets; Webster, the solemn, ever-judging cat of the bishop, brought up in a deanery, who loosens up a bit when he laps some spilled whiskey; collectors of old English silver cow-creamers; constables on bicycles; university students stealing policemen's helmets on a dare; and on and on.

The plots are as twisted and magnificently convoluted as some daytime soap opera. (Wodehouse watched *The Edge of Night* every day that he could when in America.) Rare is the chapter that doesn't end with a bang or a surprise. And, a great measure of comfort, the plots are evergreen: Bertie manages to get engaged to a completely unsuitable woman, one who has plans to stiffen his spine and make something of him, probably one who reads her own poetical effusions to him; he can't escape the woman's toils, for he is an English gentleman; knots mount up, ever more Gordian; Jeeves, who eats a lot of fish and has brains to spare, exacts a promise from Bertie that he will stop wearing that wretched tie, that moth-eaten moustache, that plaid vest, or that he will take Jeeves on holiday to the sunny Mediterranean; Jeeves, with a soupçon of dishonest maneuvering and carefully placed less-than-truths, saves the day. There will be joy in the morning.

Or Connie, yet again, hires as Clarence's secretary the once-dispelled Efficient Baxter; Clarence doesn't WANT a secretary, prefers to potter about and read books on how many calories a fat pig needs per day; but Connie prevails; cutting to the chase, Connie ends up shooting the Efficient Baxter in the bum with her grand-nephew's air rifle.

As delicious as all this is, it's the language that is the crème de la crème in Wodehouse. It's a rare page in his books that doesn't have one brand-new "I'll remember this 'un the rest of my life" simile, comic expression, or mangled and twisted cliche made brand-new.

Here's a random sampling of pure Wodehousiana taken from here and there in his oeuvre: [1] "Smedley is a poor sheep who can't say boo to a goose." "Well, name three sheep who can." [2] "Unseen, in the background, Fate was quietly slipping the lead into the boxing-glove." [3] "He talks French with both hands." [4] "The temperature dropped noticeably. A snail that was passing at the time huddled back into its shell with the feeling that there was quite a nip in the air these mornings, and would have slapped its ribs, if it had had any." [5] "Foggy between the ears." [6] "Oofy Prosser declined to be my banker, as did my banker." [7] "'Well, I think I'll mooch along and have a cup of tea,' he said, and mooched, as foreshadowed." [8]"He drank coffee with the air of a man who regretted it was not hemlock." [9] "It is never difficult to distinguish between a Scotsman with a grievance and a ray of sunshine." [10] "He was in the acute stage of that malady which, for want of a better name, scientists call the heeby-jeebies." [11] "It's an iron-clad contract, and if she attempts to slide out of it, she'll get bitten to death by wild lawyers." [12] "One prefers, of course, on all occasions to be stainless and above reproach, but, failing that, the next best thing is unquestionably to have got rid of the body." [13] "He strode off into the darkness, full to the brim with dudgeon." [14] "His reputation is that of a man who, if there are beans to be spilled, will spill them with a firm and steady hand. He has never kept a secret and never will. His mother was frightened by a BBC announcer." [15] "Lord Emsworth had one of those minds capable of accommodating but one thought at a time--if that." [16] "I was behind the desk, crouching on the carpet and trying to breathe solely through the pores." [17] "If not actually disgruntled, he was far from being gruntled." [18] "Gussie, a glutton for punishment, stared at himself in the mirror." [19] "My earnest hope is that the entire remainder of my existence will be one round of unruffled monotony." [20] "I can't stand Paris. I hate the place. Full of people talking French, which is a thing I bar. It always seems to me so affected." [21] "Inherited wealth, of course, does not make a young man nobler or more admirable, but the young man does not always know this." [22] "I am told by one who knows that hens cannot raise their eyebrows, not having any; but I am prepared to swear that at this moment this hen raised hers. I will go further. She sniffed." [23] "I don't know whether I am standing on my head or my heels." "Sift the evidence. At which end of you is the ceiling?" [24] "He danced like something dark and slithery from the Argentine." [25] "Like all Baronets, he had table-thumping blood in him."

There's no end to Wodehouse's quotability. So I'll just quit.

"Nice" Used To Be an Insult

[Adapted from material in my book *Word Study*.]

No language stands still, except a dead one. If a tongue is spoken, if it is written, it is mutable. If academies are founded with the hope of impeding such change, how mostly futile the hope. Words are deflected from their original sense for inevitable reasons: the extension of knowledge, the caprice of choice from a capacious vocabulary, changes in fashion, metaphorical twists, social changes of all kinds, and jocular or sober ignorance.

Linguists focus on two pairs of changes in word meanings: degeneration and its less-common opposite, elevation; and generalization and its opposite, specialization.

A word's meaning may be said to degenerate when it becomes weaker or signifies something less agreeable or less respectable. Disparagement of social groups other than one's own is a major cause of word degeneration. Those of high social rank and those who wield the pen wield linguistic power. Early farmers rarely wrote; see what happens. *Villain* is from the French for a peasant, a country laborer; *boor* is from the Dutch for farmer; *clown* ultimately derives from the Latin for a country laborer, a rustic. The villain's, boor's, and clown's "social betters" suggest that the peasant is an unprincipled scoundrel, a rude and ill-mannered person, a clumsy simpleton; the process of degeneration is off and running.

Natural pessimism is a second force in degeneration. That we tend to expect and believe the worst is shown in the word *criticize*. Everyone's first thought is that the verb means to show the negative points of—not to weigh both pluses and minuses. Similarly, the Greek word for "actor" was *hypocrite*, someone under (*hypo*) criticism. Everyone knows what *hypocrite* means today, a great degeneration from its meaning of "performer." *Doom*, meaning a legal judgment or decree (allied to the word *deem*), comes to mean ruin, tragedy, condemnation, or death. *Silly*, meaning good, innocent, blessed, progresses past "simple" to mean merely "simpleminded." *Smug*, meaning trim, tidy, or neat, shows that spruceness stirs in the onlooker the suspicion that the spruce person is complacent or self-satisfied. The negative overpowers the positive, obliterates the dispassionate idea.

In elevation, the meaning of a word grows stronger, more agreeable, or more respectable. In social respect, for example, *minister* has been elevated. No one thinks of "servant" anymore when hearing the word. *Nice* was once a catch-all word for negatives--foolish, stupid, strange, lazy, wanton, reluctant. Now, of course, it is a catch-all, thus colorless, positive. We see intermediate meanings of "fastidious" (as in the proverbial 16th-century expression "as nice as a nun's hen" and in my own mother's rebuke of "Oh, don't be so nasty nice" when I was being squeamish about a bit of interesting nastiness) and "precisely discriminating" (as in Alexander Pope's "In the nice bee, what sense so subtly true/ From pois'nous herbs extracts the healing dew?"). The change, the elevation, from "stupid" and "lascivious" to "good" and "decent" is scarcely credible but clearly true from all of the written contexts.

In generalization, a word becomes broader and more diffused in meaning. The chief cause of generalization is doubtless the human tendency toward inexact thinking. We blur distinctions by thinking vaguely or indefinitely. Thus a *quarantine* comes to mean something other than forty days, and to decimate is not necessarily to select one out of every ten. Figurative use swells the ranks of generalization: what was a trope becomes literal. A *pioneer* was originally a member of an army's vanguard, building roads and bridges. Anyone in the forefront of advances is today's pioneer, a short leap into the figurative. Often, generalization shows the uses and customs of the past, a fossil of history. The belief in astrology is enshrined in our words *lunatic* (a moon-mad person) and *influence/influenza* (a flowing in of power from the stars to affect human beings).

In specialization, a broad meaning contracts to a narrower; the general becomes limited. Pristine ignorance restricts a word to a group's own interests, its own experience. *Starving* becomes a special kind of death, from hunger, rather than any kind of dying (as in the German *sterben*).

When Chaucer says that Jesus starved upon the cross, we pause. The trope at the heart of the Judaeo-Christian tradition turns pastor from a literal shepherd into the keeper of the flock of the faithful. And imprecise thinking limits *charity*, making it not all sorts of care and loving-kindness but just a handout. And so it goes.

Such changes as these make the reading of olden literature difficult for the unwary, for one startled by finding a character in Defoe praising a woman for being a "good hussy" (housewife) of the money he left her, or jarred by discovering in William Langland that *girl* means boy and in Chaucer *girl* means a young person of either sex. The alternative to such changes is linguistic stagnation and death. What philosophers and poets say is true: nothing is strictly immutable except mutability.

No English Academy

[Written for *Gramma*.]

"Though I cough, I plough through the rough." This sentence amply illustrates the anomalies of English spelling. Many people have felt that English spelling warrants a zeal to reform, perhaps a John Calvin of orthography. Let's query whether the obvious good so intimated is a specious good.

Surely it would be a good pure and simple not to use *-ough* to spell five different sounds, as in the opening sentence? And yet, and yet . . . .

Let me be as nearly unequivocal as an English teacher can be: On the whole, English spelling reform is a bad idea. Oh, I have fretted, fumed, and fussed with the best of the Lucy van Pelts of the world, even about spelling, not so much for myself as for my students. But it's the quick, surface thought that denounces English spelling as a hideous perversity. Extended thought concludes that the best answer to a reformer's zeal is to smile deprecatingly and indulgently, shake one's head sagely, and say, "Yes, it's a mess, but let's just leave it that way."

Not that I think the spellings *tho* and *thru*, though they look like Freewayese, do much to rend the fabric of humanity's moral existence. Words are words still. You would still be you. Or yu wud stil be yu.

Still, the student of language and literature has lost something in losing *though* and *through*. The student loses a sense of the history and heritage of the language, not seeing that Germanic words that once pronounced the end sounds encountered French, encountered English illiteracy, and altered. Nor would the student perceive that *through* and *thorough* are at base the same word, once they are altered to *thru* and *thoro*. What then happens to Andrew Marvell's lines in "To His Coy Mistress"?

Let us roll all our strength and all
Our sweetness up into one ball,
And tear our pleasures with rough strife
Thorough the iron gates of life.

Connections in meaning often count for more than does spelling convenience.

Many an average speaker of English, I know, would be willing to leave Geoffrey (strange spelling!) Chaucer and Andrew Marvell to the specialists. But reform the spelling thoroughly, that is, through and through, and Shakespeare's plays all will have to be put into the new orthography. Many subtleties of language and wordplay will be utterly lost, except to the specialist. The specialist would still read Shakespeare in the 16th- and 17th-century versions, as one in a million can still read the 10th-century language of the much earlier *Beowulf* with some pleasure, and as rather more can still derive pleasure from Chaucer's Middle English.

Of course the billions (literally) of books already in modern English would eventually be put into the new orthography, and Shakespeare and Mark Twain would be read, after a fashion. It's hard to imagine how the dialect of Twain's Huck Finn would have much point once everything is rendered phonetically. Shakespeare would be further impeded by notes to explain the point of what once were eye-rhymes, such as *move* and *love*.

In short, language is much more than just the sound a word makes as pronounced--pronounced variously, by the way.

Difficulties arise. First, we need twenty-plus new symbols to spell the English sounds that the Roman alphabet cannot adequately represent. Then we need to settle all the criteria of correct pronunciation. If the ideal of a phonetic orthography is to have one symbol represent one sound, then we need different symbols for the *a* in *cake* and the *a* in *mama*. Then if I say *tomayto* and you say *tomahto*, shall we call the whole thing off?

No one criterion of correct pronunciation exists. Samuel Johnson's *Dictionary of the English Language* fixed most English spelling principles today represented. Yet Boswell tells us that Johnson pronounced with a broad Staffordshire dialect. He said "poonsh" for *punch*. If Johnson had entered the definition for *punch* under the spelling poonsh, would Boswell (a Scot and therefore very careful about English pronunciation to escape ridicule) have called it anything but "punch"?

Regional pronunciation changes. Do we gear our spelling to chase after the variations? Do we delude ourselves that spelling would fix pronunciation? What about the wantonness of caprice? No one says it better than Johnson himself: "Much less ought our written language to comply with the corruptions of oral utterance, or copy that which every variation of time or place makes different from itself, and imitate those changes which will again be changed, while imitation is employed in observing them."

Since Johnson's day, Noah Webster has been the most famous spelling reformer. Thank him, if you are of a mind to, for divorcing American and British practice in *-our* endings. Though Webster's vanity arrogated praise to himself for petty reforms, we may question whether the international rancor caused by so small a reform is outweighed by *glamor, ardor,* and *honor.*

Let us do what we can to regularize the spelling of new words as they are introduced into the language. No use in confounding confusion well entrenched. But root-and-branch orthographic reform remains a bad idea whose time, if it ever was, has long gone. Let the French Academy struggle to control French; the English do things differently. Johnson hoped that if an English academy were ever established, the spirit of English liberty would hinder or destroy it. The spirit of English liberty, conservatism, hatred of inconvenience, or sloth--something--has so far frustrated the brave-new-spelling-world schemes of Noah Webster, George Bernard Shaw, and Teddy Roosevelt. So, let's hope, with the reforming zeal of Miss Groby, who counts spelling all, and Prof. Dinglehooper, who wouldn't mind some loss of Shakespeare to all except the specialists-in-training who butter his toast.

Is There Any Such Word As Slickery?

[Written for the newspaper column "Grammarphone."]

On Grammarphone, Frostburg State University's writer's hotline, we got this question: "On television I hear an ad that describes a throat lozenge as *slickery*. Is there any such word?"

The dictionaries don't have it, and I doubt that they ever will, but of course it's a word, a nonce word--one made up for the occasion. To make up words as we want is a fundamental human right and inclination--anything from the cry of comic lament *great googlie-mooglies* to Edmund Spenser's *braggadocio*. Some of the coined words, like *slickery*, fill no crying need and quickly fade into oblivion. Others, like *braggadocio*, fill a verbal or imaginative need, and people remember them. Dictionaries, of course, register the assent of people—the vote of use--when a word fills a need.

A number of words formed in the manner of *slickery* (*slick* + *slippery*) join two previous words together and manage to survive the years and the poppy of oblivion. Lewis Carroll called them portmanteau words because they pack a great deal of meaning, two in one suitcase. His *chortle* has made the dictionary, a blend of *chuckle* and *snort* to describe an exact kind of laugh, something like Miss Piggy would emit. Linguists call words of this sort *blends*. *TIME* magazine pushes the practice far into the realm of Cutesie-Pie Land with blends like *cinemactress* and *yellocution*.

Still, many respectable words began this way: few people wince anymore at blend-words like *smog* (*smoke* + *fog*), *motel* (*motor* or *motorist* + *hotel*) and *brunch* (*breakfast* + *lunch*). *Broasted* may not win customers by combining images of broiling and roasting, but I like the Americanism *squinch*--to pucker and pinch up the eyes or face more than a mere squint. Uglier words like *urinalysis* and *electrocute* are blends too.

The practice of blending is especially common in recent years. *Medicare* is easy to say and instantly comprehensible. Walter Winchell's *infanticipate* was not easy and is probably useless outside of gossip columns. *Anecdotage,* to describe the ever-returning jests or the dotage manifested in repeating the same old wheezes, may survive. Yet *TIME* magazine can't expect Americans to use *cinemactor* when they, sensibly, continue to prefer *movies* to *cinema*. Advertising will still try to foist *fantabulous* and *slickery* on us, but if the word is gush we will probably reject it.

Not Here, Not Now

[A poem written for my partner, Mack Lovelace.]

All we are is dust in the wind.
But that's not here, and that's not now.
Here we are pulsing flesh;
Now we are throbbing minds.
What if both the flesh and mind
Ache now and then?
The pain is heavenly hurt
When allied with love's joy.
I want no other being,
But I want _this_ being--
Sensuous, full, entwined,
Radiantly alive.

Got Me Some New Tires

[I wrote this piece in 2001, approximately one year after retiring from college teaching, for publication in *Afterword*, the quarterly of Frostburg State University's English Department.]

So far, the sternest test of my retirement has been the two bitterly cold months from mid-November to mid-January 2000/2001. Mired in the dregs of winter so soon, I wanted to sit inside, feed the fire, grow fat and lazy, and watch Maryland Public Television in the early afternoon. Curse PBS for its anglophile days. Two half-hour episodes of the British *Antiques Roadshow* gave me the chance to lust after the simple perfection of 18th-century furniture, everything I like evaluated at 10,000 pounds. Every place visited that I had seen before I wanted to see again. Every place not yet seen I wanted to see.

And then the comfort of *Last of the Summer Wine*, a mediocre comedy with the same plot every show but wonderful characters, the women observing the defects of Yorkshire men, commenting; the men walking and walking about the second-loveliest region of England. Next the fifth re-run of *As Time Goes By*, to my mind the best of the British comedies, allowed me to see Judi Dench again as she was before she became a dame, and Geoffrey Palmer, still attaining his full complement of jowliness.

Was this any way for a rational creature to live? The answer must be "Yes," since I'm not embarrassed to admit my days of huffing the fumes of English breakfast tea, having just one more cookie, then some buttered toast to cut the sweet taste, then a piece of fruit to moisten my mouth, then a few almonds to be cracked out of their shells. . . . I wonder how many cups of tea Samuel Johnson would have sucked down in a day of British television.

My body had a mind of its own and wanted to weigh 170 pounds. Now I know it's better for me, at my stature, to weigh 160 pounds, and in the summer I sometimes do, but my body wanted to weigh 170 and would not be nay-said. Fortunately, my body wanted to weigh precisely 170: I have to struggle to go beyond that mark. [Not anymore, 2019.]

I told myself that I had stored up a certain measure of allowed sloth, a counterpoise to the weight of pious industry. Had I not taught college for 34 years, since I was 22 and more callow than my students? Had I not resisted the temptation to yell "I've been teaching you what a comma splice is for 34 years; why the hell don't you know?" Had I not been in school for 51 years, the very pulse of my year beating to the school seasons?

Had I not just built the shell of a vacation home in Emory, Virginia, mostly with my own hands, often working by myself, sagging into bed most nights with aching muscles and joints, the trapezius on the left side of my neck an aching cord of over-compensation for my frozen left shoulder syndrome (coming near the end of my teaching, apparently from nothing but my having lived past five decades)?

Did I not cook dinner nearly every night? Did I not pamper our cats, holding our near-perfect cat, Dmitri, until I grew numb so that he could sleep upright like a baby in the crook of my arm? Was I not clearing out the junk of 26 years from our basement and negotiating the war-zone landscape of crusty ice and mud as we had major surgery done on our house's foundation? Did I not read about as much as ever? What a good lad was I. What a reservoir of merit!

Still, there's no denying it: I was becoming a three-toed sloth. Any day now I would discover moss growing on my back, fingering it, saying "The color isn't bad; makes a nice change."

I knew, before retiring, the three absences that would gape the widest: the daily camaraderie of my friends; the pleasure of knowing most students-- young, generous, and most of them sweet; and the exhilaration of the stage of the classroom on the best days, when just the right mix of planning and impromptu gave us *théatre vivant.*

My friends I see often, and the camaraderie is still natural and lively, even to the trading of insults on others' tastes and politics. Their daily concerns, however, are no longer my daily concerns; but I knew they wouldn't be and have fortified myself against that difference as well as I can. New faces are rapidly changing the old comfortable people-scape.

What to do to replace the sweetness of students I do not well know. I continue friendships and correspondences with some, but it's not the same, everybody knows.

What I will do to replace the passion and dynamism of the classroom these musings may help me to discover. Not all passion is spent, but I am somewhat, a little, advanced into the sere and yellow leaf; less will do me. I will do a bit of writing, which is, if not a paroxysm of creation, something suited to the gentle slope into the vale. I find that words flow pretty much in the same way as before, once I can coax myself to the desk. I always felt guilty teaching students to write many drafts and edit, edit, edit. I still compose in my head and write one draft, fiddling with it scarcely a jot. As Byron said, the pleasure is having written. For creativity I will also have almost two acres, nearly flat, in the sunshine at Emory, enough room for 12-foot-deep flower borders, teaching the admiring multitudes what horticultural bliss is.

Any road, as the Yorkshiremen say, I know that my sense of accomplishment as a teacher was inflated. One sees stacks of papers graded and understandably confuses the tangible with the real. If I have racked up three inches of paper-grading, then I have accomplished real work. Maybe. If I can keep my liberty from turning into license, it's good to have a life, a-nights and all, weekends free of papers. I struggle to regain that carefree obliviousness to time, which I had as a child, before being cursed by timepieces. I've not brought myself to shed my watch yet, but I will manage to look at it less. And if I become a sloth in winter, don't lots of creatures do so? A comatose cat in the sun on a window-sill--one could do worse for a model of deep-down nature.

Love Poems for Mack

[Below are three poems, mostly light, written for Mack early on.]

Let's Make It Fly

"Lord, he makes a good blackberry pie,"
You said to your beloved aunt,
And it warmed my heart.
That you like fruit pie and real whipped cream
I take for a rousing good sign.
You might not like cheese;
Take or leave avocado;
And your stand on artichokes
Is nothing short of appalling.
But you're sound on fruit pie and whipped cream,
The real *sine qua non.*
So this thing just might fly.

Decoction

Lust is a complex brew, God knows--
As serious as Schopenhauer,
As ditzy as Gracie Allen.
Sapient Will knew about lust:
"Mad in pursuit and in possession so."
But did he mean man-lust too?
Maybe he did.
I'm sure that he felt it,
All-embracing Will.
And love?
It's as complex as lust,
Maybe even moreso.
Explain it in light vein I cannot.
We need a Gregory Corso.

Bright Passage

If the passage of time meant merely loss,
Loss of a few days of what we have,
Denied a few crumbs from tables high,
It were a dark passage indeed.

But John Donne was right:
"Inter-assurèd of the mind,
We care less eyes, lips, and hands to miss."
Not that we care none--
Far from it.
But see how love has grown
Apart from each other.
Apart, but linked in pledge and longing.
Time's passage clarifies the mind:
We know we want each other,
For the good the other brings.
And for the bad?
Who can avoid it and live?

Two More Poems for Mack

Reverdie

There came a day in early spring,
Buds and blooms still dormant,
That showed me, late but true,
How to sing "Spring-a-ding-ding,
Everything grows anew."
Chaucer sang it so:
"When April with its sweet showers . . . ."
And the Pearl Poet also:
"The cold ebbs and declines,
The clouds lift. . . ."
But mine was a spiritual green,
The sweet showers of vernal hope,
The lifting clouds not masking joy.
What happened that turned March
To soft-winged summer,
Freighted with music and fragrance?
I spent some days with you,
And all was green and gold,
Smelling of dew
And rain
And earth.

Hi-Ho

I like that you sing as you work,
Whether straightening up
Your mess upstairs
Or mine down in the scullery,
Like a holy madman as you mow
Or as you potter about,
Moving to and fro.
Such continuing cantabile
Tells me that you are happier than you think.
My mother sang so,
And she had the gift of cheer.
I wish I could lay
That flattering unction to my soul
That you're happy because you're around me.
I won't say you're not,
But to say that's all
Is just not so:
You're happier than you know.

Renaissance and Renascence

[This is a long paper written for publication and a trans-Atlantic videoconference celebrating the joint centenaries of Frostburg State University and Mary Immaculate College in Limerick, Ireland, where I taught for one semester. I compare the glories of the literatures of the American South and of Irish literature in English, primarily in the twentieth century.]

From the Southern Literary Renascence, hear the words of glorious excess: Faulkner's Gavin Stephens characterizes the South absolutely and hyperbolically: "The past is never dead. It's not even past." Robert Penn Warren speaks sweepingly when he says that the Southern writer "has to feel about his country the same way he feels about his mother. He loves her but she annoys him to death." In the vulgarian vein, the narrator of Eudora Welty's "Why I Live at the P. O." explains in extraordinarily compressed language "Papa-Daddy's Mama's papa and sulks." Ratcheting the rhetoric quite a few notches higher, Thomas Wolfe has George Webber conclude *You Can't Go Home Again* with a letter to his friend Fox Edwards:

> Something has spoken to me in the night, burning the tapers of the waning year; something has spoken in the night, and told me I shall die, I know not where. Saying: "To lose the earth you know, for greater knowing; to lose the life you have, for greater life; to leave the friends you loved, for greater loving; to find a land more kind than home, more large than earth-- Whereon the pillars of this earth are founded, toward which the conscience of the world is tending--a wind is rising, and the rivers flow."

To this rhetoric of abstraction add Zora Neale Hurston's rhetoric of concreteness:

> It was the time for sitting on porches beside the road. It was the time to hear things and talk. These sitters had been tongueless, earless, eyeless conveniences all day long.

Mules and other brutes had occupied their skins. But now, the sun and the bossman were gone, so the skins felt powerful and human. They became lords of sounds and lesser things. They passed nations through their mouths. They sat in judgment.

Excessive? Yes. But glorious? Indubitably.

From the Irish Literary Renaissance, hear the words of glorious excess: Synge's dialogue between Lucifer and a Lost Soul explains the mystery of how a good lad comes to be in hell:

> Lucifer: And what brought you this place?
> Lost Soul: The way of the world, your reverence.
> Lucifer: Bad company.
> Lost Soul: The worst. In Maynooth I was with all nice little priests, talking ever and always of the deadly merits. I run from that.

In the extravagance of the regional speech of Kiltartan, County Galway, Lady Gregory portrays one pauper, Mike McInerney, justifying his dogs' having bitten another inmate of the workhouse ward, Michael Miskell: "Thinking you were a wild beast they did, that had made his escape out of the travelling show, with the red eyes of you and the ugly face of you, and the two crooked legs of you that wouldn't hardly stop a pig in a gap." James Stephens, loosely translating a 17th-century poem in Irish, pulls out all of the stops for an occasion meriting rhetorical excess--a barmaid's refusing the "loan" of a glass of beer:

> That parboiled ape, with the toughest jaw you will see
> On virtue's path, and a voice that would rasp the dead,
> Came roaring and raging the minute she looked at me . . . .

James Joyce succinctly but hyperbolically sums up Ireland: "There is no Christian love in Ireland. There are too many Protestants and Catholics." Add Yeats's unforgettable portrait of the skeletal, decayed beauty of an aged Maude Gonne:

Did Quattrocento finger fashion it
Hollow of cheek as though it drank the wind
And took a mess of shadows for its meat?

Excessive? Yes. But glorious? Indubitably.

Accused of rhetorical excess, both the American Southern writer and the Irish might respond that in their regions of the world a paradox is a fitting motto: Too much is just about enough. Chided that such extravagance is not realistic, the writers of both regions can respond, "Oh, but it is." What's the great difference between Welty's "Papa-Daddy's Mama's papa and sulks" and the linguistic daring that one can hear from any old Southern woman tired of life and satisfied that she has done the best she could with what was given: "I've done done my do"? The old woman, a perceptive though uneducated linguist, knows that English communicates grammar primarily by where words are; thus <u>do</u> is a noun, just as <u>sick</u> is a noun in Hurston's "Not the dead of sick and ailing with friends at the pillow and the feet." Or how is the extravagance of Stephens's Irish curse any more hyper-real than the folk-saying of contempt "I wouldn't be seen dead at a pig fair with him"? Or the paradoxical truth of the Kerryman in *Our Like Will Not Be There Again* who says in open conversation, "Listening to me friends was all the reading that ever I done in my life."

Still, how provincial. How place-ridden, idiosyncratic, and insular to take the speech of an ignorant, spiteful, self-justifying autochthon of China Grove, Mississippi ("Not that it isn't the next to smallest P. O. in the entire state of Mississippi") and hope that the rest of the world will see something enduring in "Papa-Daddy will certainly beat you on the head if you come within forty miles of him. He thinks I deliberately said he ought to cut off his beard after he got me the P. O., and I've told him and told him and told him, and he acts like he just don't hear me. Papa-Daddy must of gone stone deaf." And how can Lady Gregory have hoped to make something enduring from the notorious logorrhea of a small place in a then-depopulated county, in a tiny country on the fringes of Europe? When Michael Miskell is challenged to prove that the Miskells have as great name as the McInerneys, he responds, "Go across to Lisheen

Crannagh and down to the sea and to Newtown Lynch and the mills of Duras and you'll find a Miskell . . . ." Oh, I see, the big world.

But the very provincialism of the Irish Literary Renaissance and the American Southern Renascence is the source of the literatures' universality. The two literatures have made pre-eminent contributions to the literature of the world by their insistently concrete view of a real place--of its physical substance and narrowness. Out of this critical social realism, this self-consciousness, has sprung profound philosophical truth--universal abstraction derived from the insistence on the concrete, the particular, the known.

From the emphasis on precise social rituals and codified behavior--the oral tradition of manners--both the Irish and Southern writer gains a love of words, a love both subtle and obvious, that leads to universal stylistic innovations. The social code demands elaborate responses, straining the forces of language--the strain the mother of invention.

Most non-native travelers in the American South notice a more elaborate spoken response to queries than can be found elsewhere in this country. Lee Pederson argues that this reliance on the spoken word more than the written word is perhaps attributable to the homogeneous nature of the South at the beginning of the twentieth century, as opposed to the North, where a great many immigrants had English only as a second language and learned to be more comfortable in the language as written. The genius of the writers of the Southern Renascence was to perceive that the elaborate language of the folk, even when utterly unlettered, was a perfect literary English, not just in dialogue faithfully realistic to character but also in the author's own voice. For instance, Mary Hood, writing in *Harper's*, points out the Southerner's tendency to make an "essay response" to a simple query:

> Suppose a man is walking across a field. To the question, "Who is that?" a Southerner would reply: "Wasn't his granddaddy the one whose dog and him got struck by lightning on the steel bridge? Mama's third cousin--dead

before my time--found his railroad watch in that eight-pound catfish's stomach the next summer just above the dam. The way he married for that new blue Cadillac automobile, reckon how come he's walking like he has on Sunday shoes, if that's who it is, and for sure it is." A Northerner would reply to the same question, "That's Joe Smith." To which the Southerner might think (but be much too polite to say aloud), "They didn't ask his name—they asked who he is!"

Anyone who has ever asked such a question of an old-timey Southerner can vouch for the accuracy of the anecdote. Anyone who has ever struggled with the labyrinthine narration of Faulkner in certain complex parts of his stories can see that he is merely extending an indigenous way of talking. He hasn't invented Faulknerese from scratch. The "essay response" of not just his dialogue but also of his usual elaborate narration, substantially new in literature but not in Southern speech, has become a common stylistic trait of writers of the twentieth century, some of them imitating Faulkner, with varying degrees of success.

A different habit of Southern speech, tied to a ritualized code of manners, is to euphemize and hyperbolize in insults, striking and reining in at the same time. One cannot directly call a relative, even one by marriage, not blood, slow or stupid. So Southerners adapt the rhetorical technique akin to litotes that we see in Eudora Welty's short story "The Wide Net." A husband talks about his wife and her family: "She's a lot smarter than her cousins in Beula. And especially Edna Earle, that never did get to be what you'd call a heavy thinker. Edna Earle could sit and ponder all day on how the little tail of the 'C' got through the 'L' in a Coca-Cola sign." The ironic negative understatement--"never did get to be what you'd call a heavy thinker"--carries on the technique that the author of *Beowulf* would recognize but updates it in a way that modern realistic novelists can use.

The whole range of classical rhetoric, Homeric figures even, will be freshened or made new by the Southern writer's paying attention to the code of ritualized speech. Nothing is more characteristically Southern than the tendency to speak in elaborate figurative language, especially similes. True, cliches abound, but so do new turns of phrase, nonce similes, that extend and extend similitudes to get the precise communication of what something is like. Eudora Welty shows in "Lily Daw," as usual, absolutely perfect ear in translating this provincial way of speaking into subtle literature, even in the authorial voice that narrates: "While they rode around the corner Mrs. Carson was going on in her sad voice, sad as the soft noises in the hen house at twilight." Anyone the world over who is acquainted with chickens knows Mrs. Carson's voice. Quick and subtle metaphors supplement the similes. In Welty's short story "The Hitch-Hikers" the character called merely the guitar player complains about the music blaring from every radio: "Same songs ever'where. I come down from the hills. . . . We had us owls for chickens and fox for yard dogs but we sung true. . . . My ma, she was the one for ballats. Little in the waist as a dirt-dauber, but her voice carried. Had her a whole lot of tunes. Long ago dead an' gone. Pa'd come home from the courthouse drunk as a wheelbarrow, and she'd just pick up an' go sit on the front step facin' the hill an' sing. Ever'thing she knowed, she'd sing. Dead an' gone, an' the house burned down." The wonderful precision and surprise of "owls for chickens and fox for yard dogs" and the image of a drunk weaving along like a badly trundled wheelbarrow establish absolute fidelity to how certain uneducated Southerners talk.

How Southern Blacks talk is closely akin to how other Southerners talk, but subtle differences arise especially in the rituals of how one Black talks to another. Nobody before Zora Neale Hurston knew so much of this code of talk while having the genius to turn it to literature new under the face of the sun. She knew the code by growing up in an all-Black town, Eatonton, Florida, and by doing important research in anthropology and Black folklore. She knows, for instance, the emphatic rhythm of cadence groups that rise to the tongues of gossips: "She ain't even worth talkin' after. She sits high, but she looks low." No stress marks are needed to highlight high and low: the reader punches the words up automatically. Hurston also knows the lyricism demanded in emphatic Black talk, often achieved by alliteration and redundancy that no one wishes away: "It's sort of duskin' down dark." We can catalogue hundreds of instances of the Southern Black code of ritualized speech turned into literature by sweeping through Hurston's *Their Eyes Were Watching God*, but a dozen or so will have to suffice.

Quite common is the practice of linguistic substitution, turning a word into a different part of speech by putting it in a different sentence-position. Pheoby [*sic*] apologizes to Janie, "Mah mulatto rice ain't so good dis time. Not enough bacon grease, but Ah reckon it'll kill hongry." Once English lost nearly all of its inflections during the Norman period, this kind of substitution became the special genius of English, but Southern Black speech avails itself of the strength especially. Other quick illustrations are ". . . doin' from can't see in de mornin' till can't see at night"; "all he do is big-belly round and tell other folks whut tuh do"; "uh lavish uh talk"; and "feeds 'im offa 'come up' and seasons it wid raw-hide."

Linguistic inventiveness also surfaces in coinages, especially pseudo-Latin words that show that lack of education will not impede poetic license: "Time makes everything old so the kissing, young darkness became a monstropolous old thing while Janie talked"; "Ah'll take a stick and salivate 'im!"; "'Scuse mah freezolity"; "set you down on yo' royal diasticutis'" and "protolapsis uh de cutinary linin.'" The code demands vivid language, and the context is gloss enough.

The vividness of Southern Black metaphor shows no real difference in kind from the metaphors of other Southern speech patterns but a shade of difference in degree. Both are derived from the impulse to make abstractions clear in living terms, but Black speech—and therefore writing drawing its inspiration from this speech—draws, sometimes, on metaphors akin to folk proverbs slightly different from the world observed by, say, Eudora Welty. This striving-for-the-pith-of proverbs way of speaking is shown in Hurston's "They don't know if like is a mess of corn-meal dumplings, and if love is a bed-quilt"; "livin' through uh hundred years in January without one day of spring"; "Some people could look at a mud-puddle and see an ocean with ships" and the observation that the earth "soaks up urine and perfume with the same indifference."

Compare these literary expressions with common Southern folk-wisdom: "Mean to don't pick no cotton"; "no more chance than a kerosene cat in hell with gasoline drawers on"; "God Almighty's overcoat wouldn't make him no vest"; and "There's more ways to kill a cat than choking it to death with butter." This last *sententia* might have been drawn from the pages of many a Southern writer, but it is in fact drawn from the everyday speech of my mother. The code demands that gnomic wisdom be delivered at a remove or two from the abstract. Never mind that as an eight-year-old I wasn't certain exactly what my mother was saying.

If I remove the dialect markers from Hurston, can you tell which of the following figures are from the folk, which are literary? Something is "muddy enough to bog the shadow of a buzzard"; "faces becoming sharp enough to hew their own coffins"; someone aspiring above himself: "He's got a low eye for a high fence"; and "He's a mean old hound dog that wouldn't bother to scratch his mamma's fleas." Second grouping: a certain woman is "good for nothing but to break wood over her head"; "look through muddy water and see dry land"; "like seeing your sister turn into a 'gator"; and "no more business with a plow than a hog with a holiday." The first four quotations are somewhat common Southern folk expressions, not attributable to anyone, gathered by Robert Hendrickson. The second group of four are from *Their Eyes Were Watching God*. I see no difference in excellence: both groups are exquisitely expressive. Taken together, they show the realism and speech-driven art of this writer of the Southern Renascence.

Emulating the rituals of speech in literary writing necessitates an attention to rhythm beyond what we have already noted Hurston doing. Southern folk speech has a ritual of making impromptu rhyme in coda-like passages of summing-up. The rhymes may be of the breeze/trees kind reprehended by Alexander Pope, but the spontaneous rhythm- and rhyme-making is no mean feat. Hurston shows this tradition at work: "He wouldn't dig potatoes, and he wouldn't rake hay: He wouldn't take a whipping, and he wouldn't run away."

No description of Southern speech rituals would be complete without a glance at folk-manglings, malapropism arising from knowing the spoken language better than the written. I'm not sure that my mother knew that the most common word in her vocabulary of postponing an importunate child—tereckly—was an oral variant of directly. I'm sure that every Southern writer that uses the form knows that it is a variant of the dictionary word, from Hurston to Harper Lee, from Faulkner to Fred Chappell. Realism demands that they use it. Scarcely less common is the butchered form of the learned word hermaphrodite—morphodite. When Scout, of *To Kill a Mockingbird*, uses it as a term of insult, she is using the received pronunciation and the received scorn, knowing not a jot of the concept of bisexuality. Two of my mother's favorite words—touchous and proagin'—may be malapropisms long inherited, but they are literary also, by imitation. I have never found the verb to proag or progue in a dictionary, but I know exactly what it means, from contexts like "Now don't go proagin' in that closet that I just straightened out." Zora Neale Hurston also knows what the word means, as does Lee Smith writing in the 1990s. Touchous nearly duplicates the meaning of touchy, but the connotation of a persnickety, overly fastidious sensitivity was always there in my mother's correction "Don't be so almighty touchous," as it is in Jem Finch's saying that Atticus "was still touchous about us and the Radleys and it wouldn't do to push him any."

Not antonyms, certainly, hyperbole and euphemism nevertheless sum up the polar differences of rhetorical excess perhaps most common in Southern speech. Crude hyperbole slops over into gawky excess, but Southern literature emulates the grand bow-wow hyperbole of Southern speech at its richest: the "kerosene cat in hell with gasoline drawers on" finds its literary match in the comment of Joe Starks on a small place as not having enough land "to cuss a cat on without gittin' yo' mouf full of hair." The excessive restraint of euphemism gives us a range of comedy, from Sister's delicate accusation that her sister, Stella-Rondo, "told [Mr. Whitaker] I was one-sided," having one breast bigger than the other; to Sister's narration that little Shirley-T. "lost the Milky Way she ate in Cairo," where "lost" means "vomited up"; to Scout Finch's disarming the blasphemy in naming the ineffable, by inserting an epithet between syllables, "Jee crawling hova."

Southern writers expanded where literature could go, showing other writers how to go there, discovering their literary style in the codes of how Southerners talk.

As evident in the writers of the Irish Literary Renaissance as in the Southern writer is an interest in how the speech of the ordinary people can be made a vehicle for literary expression. No one seems to have made this issue more a concern than John Millington Synge, though of course Lady Gregory, James Stephens, and others, and the looming giants Yeats and Joyce, show this interest also; however, Yeats's and Joyce's language is mostly more bookish.

It is evident that Synge worked assiduously over the years of his short life to develop his "Synge-song," the lilt of his language that is both a catching and a heightening of the folk speech of Ireland, whether the English flavored by Irish grammar, locutions, and rhythms, or the Irish of Aran and the other western regions Englished more authentically the more Synge learned of the language. Whether the process is osmotic--as in Synge's listening through the floor chink to the maids at work in the cottage in Wicklow--or smells of desks and oil--Synge always studying books and languages--he learned provincial Irish English, just as Faulkner knew many levels of Mississippi English.

In an early play fragment, *A Rabelaisian Rhapsody,* Synge imagines a dialogue between Rabelais and Thomas à Kempis in heaven. Thomas is surprised to find the French smut-glutton in heaven, and a dispute follows on the relative merits of their books. Rabelais begins in bookish English but, *quelle surprise,* rises to a respectable provincial Irish rhythm: "My book is like the great sea that will drink up all the ordures of the world, and remain yet with clean lips and pure jubilant voice. Your book is a puddle, and marred forever did but an innocent cow look backward over it." I like to think that Synge, in searching for the right figure, thinks naturally enough, being Irish, of the sea and a puddle. To extend the figure, he contrasts "all of the ordures of the world" going into the sea with a cow piddling in a puddle. Not every Anglo-Irish reader in Synge's day would know what Synge and every Irish peasant knew--that cows often look back contemplatively at themselves urinating. I imagine Synge merrily shifting into an Irish idiom--"did but an innocent cow look backward over it"--as he finishes the figure with an image from the Irish countryside and mild provincial euphemism. The Irish writer, as his American fellows will do decades later, goes to the folk for speech patterns, figurative *éclaircissement*, and comic euphemism.

Gratifyingly, we find, *mutatis mutandis*, Synge's and Southern writers' folk drawing upon the same instinct for the similitude that specifies, specifies. Synge draws upon such an image for Nora's hectoring description of her husband in *The Shadow of the Glen*: "It's a queer thing to see an old man sitting up there in his bed, with no teeth in him, and a rough word in his mouth, and his chin the way it would take the bark from the edge of an oak board you'd have building a door. . . ." Compare that to the American expression "faces becoming sharp enough to hew their own coffins," cited above.

Consider also how the press of quick communication leads both the Irish and the American to omit a relative pronoun that can be easily understood, though the omission is not standard English. In Synge's usage, as in "a pack of wild girls the like of them, do be walking abroad with the peelers," he is drawing directly on Irish, not English, syntax and idiom, and not just in the omitted relative pronoun. In the American example, from the redoubtable Eudora Welty, "Many's been saved at revival, twenty-two last Sunday including a Doyle, ought to counted two," the omitted <u>who</u> shows the folk tendency to scotch superfluous words when anyone with a wit will understand the connection of the clauses. Both folk are in a time-honored tradition, as shown in the ballad "Sir Patrick Spence":

> The king has written a braid letter,
> And signed it wi' his hand,
> And sent it to Sir Patrick Spence,
> Was walking on the sand.

Clearly, the Irish and the American make the common speech of their regions the basis of their creations. Synge, as Otto Reinert notes, has a good many items specifically of the Irish language: progressive instead of simple verb forms, inversion, "illogical" coordination with <u>and</u> instead of subordination, <u>after</u> and a progressive verb instead of a perfect, <u>itself</u> for emphasis, among others. Stylistic characteristics also borrowed from Irish include very frequent similes, with metaphors rare (Shades of the American folk speech!) and "strong non-periodicity (the voice, as if self-entranced, trailing off into upbeat image or speech tag after the completion of the sense)," all peppered with "naive-solemn circumstantial concreteness." Almost every line of *The Playboy of the Western World* would illustrate these practices. By 1907 Synge had perfected his art, an art drawn from the common discourse of the unlettered.

William Butler Yeats in "The Municipal Gallery Revisited," attributed the art of the early Irish Renaissance to the Irish soil:

> John Synge, I and Augusta Gregory, thought
> All that we did, all that we said or sang
> Must come from contact with the soil, from that
> Contact everything Antaeus-like grew strong.

This assertion is more easily demonstrated in Synge and in Lady Gregory, perhaps, than in Yeats himself. Certainly, Synge and Lady Gregory spurred each other on; they seem to have emulated each other in emulating the Irish folk and their speech. Did one not know that the slam-bang attack of Mike McInerney on Michael Miskell--"the two crooked legs of you that wouldn't hardly stop a pig in a gap"--is from Lady Gregory's *Workhouse Ward*, one would surely attribute it to Synge. Still, Yeats, even in his poetry, shows an occasional folk-image as he talks about more literary matters. In "Blood and the Moon," in which he develops the symbol of his tower at Thoor Ballylee as a representation of Ireland conquered, he catalogues Irish men of letters, including Bishop Berkeley:

> . . . God-appointed Berkeley that proved all things a
> dream,

That this pragmatical, preposterous pig of a world, its
farrow that so solid seem,
Must vanish on the instant if the mind but change its
theme.

This image is of the Irish soil--a pig and its farrow--but the language
could hardly be. Still, Yeats is right: the newness of the Irish Literary
Renaissance was drawn from that which is old indeed, the language and
the oral traditions of the folk.

Such is the instinct of the unlettered that they seize on that which is
most timeless and necessary in communication. The Irish and American
Southern writers that emulate the unlettered gain the same note of
timelessness and universality.

Paradoxically, this innovation arises from two past-haunted regions. One
might say "past-blessed" and "past-cursed" also. The persistence of the
past in the present, especially in a world intent on obliterating the past, as
much of the twentieth century seemed to be, teaches what is ephemeral
and what endures, what is merely local, what is pandemically human. This
teaching, too, is a universal arising from what at first seems to be insular
and self-obsessed, narrow particulars.

Perched here on the verge of the new century, a world away in space
and time, seemingly, scarce regarding anything older than yesterday, the
American student will be puzzled by reading an unglossed text of, say,
Yeats's *Cathleen ni Houlihan*. Who is this past-obsessed woman maundering
on about how far she has wandered and how her four green fields were
taken from her? What can young Michael do about it, and what right has
she to blight the joy of a household just celebrating a good and profitable
marriage? Why spread the sulls and gloom as you go? Once the student
is made to see that the old woman, Cathleen ni Houlihan, is Ireland, and
her four green fields are Leinster, Munster, Connacht, and Ulster, the
American will probably think, "Now it makes more sense, but what's it to
me? Why don't the Irish just get over it and stop living in the past?" (The
student will of course ignore that the play dates from 1902 and that the

Irish have since regained most of the four green fields.) It is the teacher's job, of course, to try to show the universals in the eye-turned-inward play, not the least of which is that self and material gain must sometimes be subordinated to a larger good.

An Irish student, having heretofore almost nothing of a race problem in the American sense, may likewise be utterly puzzled by the rush of place-specific details of the past that haunt Isaac McCaslin in Faulkner's *Go Down, Moses.* Even if the Irish student perceives that the one of "one simple enough to believe that horror and outrage were first and last simply horror and outrage and was crude enough to act upon that" is John Brown, and then learns who John Brown is, what is the student, lost in the great ocean of Faulkner Incognita, to make of casual allusions to Jackson and Hooker, Longstreet and Ashby? And why should the student care about this self-regarding piece of provincial minutiae? Well, at least to care about the universal idea that there is no renouncing that gains freedom from the rest of the world; in the words of the often mule-headed McCaslin Edmonds, rebutting the moral complacency of Ike, "And anyway, you will be free [of the stains of the past].--No, not now nor ever, we from them [American Blacks] nor they from us."

Not even Faulkner portrays a South more driven by the echoing past than Katherine Anne Porter in *The Old Order.* Miranda recalls her grandmother (Sophia Jane) and Nanny, Sophia's ex-slave, now her dearest friend, in the early twentieth-century South: "They talked about the past, really--always about the past. Even the future seemed like something gone and done with when they spoke of it . . . . Who knows why they loved their past? It had been bitter for them both . . . ." Miranda does not understand how Nanny, born in slavery, having buried ten of her thirteen children in far-away Kentucky, and her grandmother, finding herself connected to one feckless man after another--her brother, her husband, her sons--can live so much in the past. How can her grandmother, twice a year, pore over the last few fading remnants of the romantically dead favorite daughter? And do grownups mean anything when they speak? How can her father say "There were never any fat women in the family" when Great-aunt Eliza sits "one solid pyramidal monument from floor to neck" and Great-aunt Keziah is not allowed to sit her husband's good horses once she attains 220 pounds? Romanticizing a South that never was, Miranda's family puzzle her in a place-specific obsession with the past. Still, though the rest of the world is not 1903 back-country Texas, where "the law of female decorum had teeth in it," and though the rest of the world will not be chastised for wearing jeans--"Ain't you ashamed of yo-self, Missy? It's against the Scriptures to dress like that"--universals arise so forcefully just because of these particulars. How else portray the universal delusions of family pride, gender-embitterment, and the romance of death?

Likewise, the very title of Synge's play *The Well of the Saints* shows that the play is tied to the backward-looking and peculiar landscape of Ireland. What is a skeptical, miracle-doubting Protestant American to make of this play in which a blind old man and a blind old woman are miraculously given sight again by the grace of water from a saint's well? Surely, the dramatization of the ideas that a blessing might be a curse, that a delusion is sometimes a mercy, for the old man and the old woman cannot tolerate the sight of each other once they see. This idea and others are not hedged in by the confines of place. Life is consistent.

That human life is consistently--and nobly--tragic is known as a given to Southern and Irish writers, the Southerner unable to sustain some of the illusions that drive America, the Irish not Anglo, not wholly Irish, and often not Anglo-Irish. Poverty in the midst of abundance, defeat in the midst of success, evil in the midst of fantasies of innocence and perfectibility--these educe a tragic vision. What is more universal than life as tragedy?

That soul-harrowing poverty in the midst of general abundance often generates tragedy is known to the Southern writer, a truth nearly always forgotten by the haves of the world. The American South in the 1920s clearly did not share the high-flying wealth and optimism of what must surely be the most optimistic nation to exist on the face of this earth. For the next forty years, at least, the South could be tutor to the rest of the country and the world.

Such a tutor is ancient Phoenix Jackson, of Welty's short story "A Worn Path," on the long foot-trek to get the charity medicine that will give her grandson temporary relief. She knows the ills of poverty: her grandson ate lye; periodically his throat starts to close up; she walks the miles and miles to town, leaving the child alone, back off the old Natchez Trace, to get medicine that will open his throat for a while. Were he not poor, and black also, his case might be more hopeful.

Paul Whitehurst, the central consciousness of William Styron's short story "Shadrach," in *A Tidewater Morning*, has yet to learn the troubles of poverty, how it incapacitates a man of good will. Ten years old in the summer of 1935, he scorns the "bourgeois aspirations and gentility which were [his] own inheritance, feeling "deprived of a certain depravity," longing to be downwardly mobile, like the now white-trashy Dabneys in the Virginia Tidewater--"that primordial American demesne where the land was sucked dry by tobacco, laid waste and destroyed a whole century before golden California became an idea." Now Vernon Dabney, scion of an old Virginia plantation family, cannot bury an ancient ex-slave that has trudged all the way from Alabama to die and be buried where he swam as a boy. "I ain't got thirty-five dollars! I ain't got *twenty-five* dollars! I ain't got *five* dollars!" No wonder that this good man, much marred by his poverty, curses "Franklin D-for-Disaster Roosevelt. The Dutchman millionaire. And his so-called New Deal ain't worth diddley squat." No wonder he yells, "Death ain't nothin' to be afraid about . . . .It's life that's fearsome! *Life*!"

The Irish of the close of the nineteenth century--not Lady Gregory, Synge, and Yeats, of course, all privileged--know the grip of poverty and concomitant tragedy. The honor of these privileged writers, in part, is that they got very precise about Ireland's have-nots and built enduring art from their humanity. A brief sampling of these three answers best.

An early poem of Yeats, "The Ballad of Moll Magee," tells the tragic story of a poor vagabond, wife of a fisherman:

My work was saltin' herrings
The whole of the long day.

And sometimes from the saltin' shed
I scarce could drag my feet,
Under the blessed moonlight,
Along the pebbly street.

I'd always been but weakly,
And my baby was just born;
A neighbour minded her by day,
I minded her till morn.

Exhausted ("A weary woman sleeps so hard!"), she rolls over on her newborn in her sleep and kills it. Driven from the house, cursed by her husband, she now wanders the roads, children flinging stones at her. The particulars are Irish, the grim outcome of poverty, universal.

The illiteracy that frequently accompanies poverty is partly the source of catastrophe in Lady Gregory's *The Gaol Gate.* A wife and mother come to Galway expecting their husband/son to be released from jail, finding him, instead, hanged and buried. They have with them a letter telling of his conviction, but they--illiterate both--did not pick up the letter and never asked any of their neighbors to read it once they got it. Their neighbors thought that the man had peached on his two friends in order to get free. The two women are consoled only by telling themselves of the noble name the man will have now that he has died for the crimes of two men who go free, who apparently peached on *him*. The details are County Galway, 1906, the condition, injustice for the poor.

The plot of Synge's *Riders to the Sea* is too familiar to require summary. Who, once seared by this stark tragedy of a woman's losing all of her sons to the sea, can ever forget it? Maurya's fatalism--her acceptance of the loss of everything--is timeless, though it is not always the ineluctable seas around Ireland that devour the poor.

Defeat comes in more guises than poverty, and it is most bitter when it comes in the face of others' success. Ireland in the 1890s, in the Anglo world but not quite of it, has, by any reasonable definition, known centuries of defeat, starkly contrasting with the riding-high successes of English imperialism. The South in the 1920s, uniquely defeated in the midst of American success, ground into the dirt, embittered especially by the right of their conquerors' cause, knows what the Irish know, what the world constantly denies: Misery is the lot of humanity, and life is a tragedy. Perhaps one cannot claim that the depths, the ecstasy of unsuccess created the great literatures that grew in these places, but paradoxical it certainly is.

Lyrical and lovely the early poetry of Yeats, but not until the volume *Michael Robartes and the Dancer,* not until the poems like "Easter 1916" do we see a complacent, self-congratulatory man rising to the pinnacles of his glory, echoing down the decades by making Ireland's tragedy his subject.

> I write it out in a verse--
> MacDonagh and MacBride
> And Connolly and Pearse
> Now and in time to be,
> Wherever green is worn,
> Are changed, changed utterly:
> A terrible beauty is born.

One must match a giant with a giant: I'll see your Yeats and call; I have a Faulkner. Has a torrent of rhetoric ever been so nobly used as by Faulkner in his review of the South's defeat? He describes the "Reconstruction" of the South after the Civil War:

> . . . that dark corrupt and bloody time while three separate
> peoples had tried to adjust not only to one another but
> to the new land which they had created and inherited too
> and must live in for the reason that those who had lost it
> were no less free to quit it than those who had gained it
> were:-- those upon whom freedom and equality had been
> dumped overnight and without warning or preparation

or any training in how to employ it or even just endure it and who misused it not as children would nor yet because they had been so long in bondage and then so suddenly freed, but misused it as human beings always misuse freedom . . . those who had fought for four years and lost to preserve a condition under which that franchisement was anomaly and paradox, not because they were opposed to freedom as freedom but for the old reasons for which man (not the generals and politicians but man) has always fought and died in wars: to preserve a status quo or to establish a better future one to endure for his children; and lastly, as if that were not enough for bitterness and hatred and fear, that third race even more alien to the people whom they resembled in pigment and in whom even the same blood ran, than to the people whom they did not . . . and in another generation would be engaged in a fierce economic competition of small sloven farms with the black men they were supposed to have freed and the white descendants of fathers who had owned no slaves anyway . . . (*Go Down Moses*).

These are the white Southerner, the black Southerner, and the white carpetbagger, but also humanity through all the ages, tragic in defeat.

Yet another source of tragedy, evil in the midst of fantasies of innocence, bursting that bubble of all bubbles--that human beings are perfectible creatures--calls with special force to the Irish and Southern writer. Much of the evil in Ireland's last century, delusively called innocence, has been political murder after murder after murder. Murder of the human soul through slavery has been the American South's chosen evil.

Not usually considered a part of the main Irish Literary Renaissance, through lateness, not lack of greatness, Frank O'Connor ably illustrates the peculiarly Irish tragedy. His short story "Guests of the Nation" is an account of a group of Irish soldiers having to shoot two English prisoners, their chums and card-playing mates, in reprisal for the English having shot four

Irish prisoners. A large and seemingly unending conflict is brought down to the intimately personal level. One of the English prisoners, Hawkins, says he would never shoot a pal; the other Englishman, Belcher, says, "I never could make out what duty was myself"; and the Irish narrator, Bonaparte, wishes the two prisoners would run. "I knew if they did run for it, that I'd never fire on them." But the Irish soldiers shoot the two anyway, leaving Noble and Bonaparte, the two Irish soldiers who felt real affection for their English prisoners, scarred for life. A universal soldier's dilemma and tragedy, this.

In *Go Down, Moses* Faulkner personifies the Southern evil in Lucius Quintus Carothers McCaslin, Mississippi slave-owner who begets a daughter upon his property, the slave Eunice, and then when that daughter, Thomasina, is a girl-woman, summons her to his bed and begets a child upon his own daughter, not to be acknowledged until after he is dead and gone. Old Carothers McCaslin's white grandson, Ike, renounces his patrimony, saying that God sees that all Southerners are Grandfather, the land dedicated as a refuge of liberty from the "old world's worthless twilight" "already accursed. . . already tainted even before any white man owned it by what Grandfather and his kind, his fathers, had brought into the new land . . . ." The American fantasy of liberty and innocence, peculiar to this country, part of the overall human tragedy, thus moves Faulkner to greatness.

What is more universal than life as tragedy? Life as high, though often raucous, comedy? Prodigious comic inventiveness seems the greatest gift of both Irish and Southern writers, the portraits of "orneriness and general cussedness" as the usual human character. It has been said that "the world is a comedy to those who think, a tragedy to those who feel." If so, the Irish and Southern writers both feel and think, and usually the best of both in the same writers.

The comedy of James Joyce owes much to its originating in peculiarly Irish situations; yet this comedy has universal appeal. No small measure of that comedy arises from a ghost that Flannery O'Connor found in the American South: she said that her small region of the world is

"Christ-haunted." The Ireland of Joyce is not just Christ-haunted but also Jehovah-, Catholic Church-, and priest-haunted. Thus, comedy can be derived from the flippancy and mild blasphemy of Buck Mulligan, who, hearing the milkwoman say "Glory be to God" for the lovely morning, explains to the Englishman Haines, "The islanders speak frequently of the collector of prepuces." Mulligan likes the jest so well that he repeats it to Stephen Dedalus: "Jehovah, collector of prepuces, is no more." To an outsider, this appears to be a peculiarly Irish kind of humor. I cannot imagine an American Southerner uttering the line, though of course we delight in an Irishman's uttering it.

Sometimes the comedy in Joyce is narrowly specific just because it arises from his life itself. In *A Portrait of the Artist as a Young Man* Stephen Dedalus catalogues his father's (Joyce's father's) positions: "A medical student, an oarsman, a tenor, an amateur actor, a shouting politician, a small landlord, a small investor, a drinker, a good fellow, a storyteller, somebody's secretary, something in a distillery, a taxgatherer, a bankrupt and at present a praiser of his own past." Not every nation will offer the field of opportunity for occupations afforded Mr. Dedalus, but the parents of every citizen of every nation of every age threaten to become praisers of their own past. The comedy is delightfully universal though merely autobiographical.

More often, the higher moments of Joyce's comedy arise from an idiosyncratically Irish chauvinism, discussing other--and therefore inferior—civilizations with a winning comic contempt. Professor MacHugh dismisses Rome: "What was their civilisation? Vast, I allow: but vile. Cloacae; sewers. The Jews in the wilderness and on the mountaintop said: *It is meet to be here. Let us build an altar to Jehovah.* The Roman, like the Englishman who follows in his footsteps, brought to every new shore on which he set his foot (on our shore he never set it) only his cloacal obsession. He gazed about him in his toga and he said: *It is meet to be here. Let us construct a watercloset.*"

Where two Irish hauntings meet--the conjunction of religion and the English--is where we find perhaps the most Irish, most raucous comedy in Joyce. Consider the confab in Barney Kiernan's pub. The character called "the citizen," a rabid Sinn Feinian, and his "bloody mangy mongrel," Garryowen, "the old dog at his feet looking up to know who to bite and when," possess the "gloryhole" in the pub when the unnamed, hard-drinking narrator of the Cyclops section and Joe Hynes enter. The narrator sees that the citizen is so assiduously "working for the cause" that the conversation is likely to explode at any time. He tries to steer the conversation into neutral channels, and Leopold Bloom studiously eyes spider webs or tries non sequiturs to avoid the harangue. (It's clear that the citizen hates all outsiders, Jew and English alike.) Still, there's no sidetracking the citizen. "What did those tinkers in the cityhall at their caucus meeting decide about the Irish language? . . . .To hell with the bloody brutal Sassenachs and their *patois."* When Bloom tries ameliorating words about moderation and civilization, the citizen counters with a variation of the island speciality, an Irish curse this time: "Their syphilisation, you mean. To hell with them! The curse of a goodfornothing God light sideways on the bloody thicklugged sons of whores' gets! No music and no art and no literature worthy of the name. Any civilisation they have they stole from us. Tonguetied sons of bastards' ghosts." This would be shocking had not Joyce disarmed it some with the comic buildup and the chauvinistic absurdity of the charge--the English no literature! The conversation eddies into safe channels, but the citizen will not be quieted. His intemperance heats up as the rounds of drink build up. The pub discussion moves to corporal punishment and the navy, and the citizen lashes out at the British navy: "They believe in rod, the scourger almighty, creator of hell upon earth and in Jacky Tar, the son of a gun, who was conceived of unholy boast, born of the fighting navy, suffered under rump and dozen [caning on the breech], was scarified, flayed and curried, yelled like bloody hell, the third day he arose again from the bed, steered into haven, sitteth on his beamend till further orders whence he shall come to drudge for a living and be paid." The curse and the parody of the creed are both Irish-centered in a way that the rest of the world may find requiring annotation. But the universality of lashing out at one's oppressors with every tool available, even high-flown distortion and blasphemy, raises the scene to high comedy of universal appeal.

Synge perhaps outstrips even Joyce for provincial Irish comedy that soars to empyreal heights, and *The Playboy of the Western World* is his sublimest comedy. Not that the Irish closest to the play saw much comedy in it, rioting every night of its first production in 1907. Yeats's haranguing them on their uncivilized behavior did little to help them perceive the comedy. It is doubtful that the audience heard the fine lines of Michael James Flaherty praising the flow of drink at Kate Cassidy's wake, for the catcalls and throwing of things at the stage had begun long before: "when we sunk her bones at noonday in her narrow grave, there were five men, aye, and six men, stretched out retching speechless on the holy stones." Had they heard, they would no doubt have objected to the maligning of the Irish. However, the rest of the world knows that an Irish wake includes drinking; the rest of the world finds appealing comedy in Michael James's rating a wake by the number of men spewing on the holy stones, and in such poetry, such assonance and consonance, "stretched out retching speechless on the holy stones"!

The audience thought that Synge maligned Irish womanhood. Indeed, the slamming contests between Pegeen and Widow Quin are not delicate. Scorning the widow for trying to mitch off with Christy Mahon, Pegeen rants at her, "Doesn't the world know you reared a black ram at your own breast, so that the Lord Bishop of Connaught felt the elements of a Christian, and he eating it after in a kidney stew? Doesn't the world know you've been seen shaving the foxy skipper from France for a threepenny bit and a sop of grass tobacco would wring the liver from a mountain goat you'd meet lepping the hills?" These all-too-specific details of Irish life might be denied by Synge's audience, but he has them from real events in the Dingle peninsula and elsewhere in County Kerry. He has merely transported them to County Mayo. It would not wash in middle-class Dublin, but the rest of the world sees the comedy of the rant, Pegeen fighting to keep the only likely man ever to drop down there "where you'll meet none but Red Linahan, has a squint in his eye, and Patcheen is lame in his heel, or the mad Mulrannies were driven from California and they lost in their wits."

The Irish audience in 1907 certainly failed to see comedy in the suggestion that Irish peasants would welcome, extol, and glorify a patricide. The audience would not have been pleased had they heard the finish--the Irish peasants do not exalt a patricide, only the telling of a grand account of a patricide. They prefer the words, not the deeds. Afraid of the English law backing the peelers, the whole crowd turn on Christy once he strikes his father a blow in front of them. Pegeen says, "A strange man is a marvel with his mighty talk" but "there's a great gap between a gallous story and a dirty deed." The situation is based, in its main particulars, on scrupulous research and note-taking done by Synge in the West of Ireland, and he has the Irish details right, from the depopulation of Mayo, to amused scorn for the peelers that overlook a bit of illicit liquor-making and -selling, being "decent, droughty poor fellows," to aiding criminals to escape the force of the English law. The Irish of the time may not have been amused by the picture of their Irish folk. The rest of the world has been, for the grand comic truths are there: most people long for the romantic, the exotic, but aren't sure they want it if they get it; the poor and disenfranchised bend the law and sympathize with the breaker of the law rather than the lawgiver; those who are esteemed may rise to match and overmatch the esteem heaped on them--these truths universal, among others, all showing life as a grand comedy.

Can the American South provide its share of comic idiosyncrasies for the writer to raise to the level of sublime comedy? Yes, and who better to link the two regions than the Irish-descended, Catholic-in-rural-Georgia writer (idiosyncratic enough) Flannery O'Connor? That she gets some of the same sort of comedy from her Christ- and God-haunted region as Joyce does is perhaps accidental, perhaps imitative. In *Ulysses* we hear the story of two drunks in a cemetery in the fog, looking for the grave of a friend of theirs. "One of the drunks spelt out the name: Terence Mulcahy. The other drunk was blinking up at a statue of our Saviour the widow had got put up." The second drunk speaks, "Not a bloody bit like the man. That's not Mulcahy, whoever done it." What God, not Mulcahy, looks like is the source of comedy in O'Connor's short story "Parker's Back." Parker, an unregenerate sinner, has married an ugly woman who doesn't approve of much of anything he likes, from automobiles to cussing. He thinks, " . . .

she was forever sniffling up sin. She did not smoke or dip [snuff], drink whiskey, use bad language or paint her face, and God knew some paint would have improved it." This is a peculiarly Southern Protestant type, intensely disapproving of what Parker thinks of as "color" in his life. She thinks that even churches are idolatrous. He is not sure whether she means to save him or is just a hard-thumping hypocrite. Either would account for her marrying him; he just doesn't know why he married her, except that "he couldn't have got her any other way." Since the age of fourteen, Parker has been driven to cover his body with tattoos. Sarah Ruth, of course, disapproves of this too: "At the judgement seat of God, Jesus is going to say to you, 'What you been doing all your life besides have pictures drawn all over you?'"

Parker (Obadiah Elihue) decides to win her approval by getting one more tattoo--one of God on his back. When he finally gets Sarah Ruth to open the door and let him back into the house, she responds, "God? God don't look like that!" Grotesque comedy this surely is; nobody but Flannery O'Connor in her situation in her region could have written it. Yet, the religious and the irreligious are races apart the world over. O. E. cannot understand the great "Thou shalt not" point of view; Sarah Ruth cannot understand a total want of spirituality. The conflict is ever with us; here it is a comic matter of tattoos.

Undeservedly little-known, O'Connor's story "The Enduring Chill" revolves around a common motif for her--the educated child flouting everything his or her mother stands for. Here the smug Asbury Fox, scornful of his mother, of all of her inane gabble, of her dairy farm, of the entire place where he grew up, returns from pursuing the "freer and ampler life," more artistic life in New York City. A failed playwright, he has returned to die, of a mysterious, wasting, romantic disease of a kind befitting an *artiste* amid the illiterati, as he sees them. The enduring chill is coming to get him, and he is still as mean and nasty to everyone as he ever was--to all except his mother's Negro workers on the dairy farm. The previous year he had come home to write a play about Negroes and worked in her dairy with them. Thinking to defy his mother especially by showing his equality with Randall and Morgan, he drinks a glass of warm milk from their jelly glass, flouting Randall's "She don't 'low that. That *the* thing she don't 'low." He repeats this demonstration of how they've got to think free if they want to live free, but they won't drink. Now, one year later, dying the death of the ill-fated, free-thinking Asbury scorns the medicine of Dr. Block, the local general practitioner. How can he find what New York doctors could not find? Anyway, "Art was sending him Death," just as it sent Kafka death. (He had written his mother from New York a two-notebook letter such as Kafka wrote to his father.) Well, no, Art is not sending him death; unpasteurized milk is sending him death; undulant fever--Bang's Disease in a cow--is sending him death. How humiliating; how grotesquely comic. He will not die, and he owes his life to his ignorant mother and the old country doctor. The details of the Negroes working for a bossy ignorant white woman are pure American South. The comedy of the romantic delusions of the mean-spirited quack artist and the comedy of arrogant condescension to one's spiritual betters is timeless and placeless.

In Southern writers the comedy ranges from the relatively minor Southern idiosyncrasy to the all-encompassing regional history, truer than many a historian's. In the first group we may place Faulkner's seizing upon the Southern passion for unusual, nonce names, intended as honorifics by the ignorant. I know that certain Southerners do this. Did I not go to school with the extended family of uneducated people with a 1950s movie-ruined imagination, with children whose given names were Monte Hale and Helen Hayes? And so Faulkner names the Snopeses Eck, Mink, Flem, Wall Street, Admiral Dewey, and Montgomery Ward.

In the second group we may place the whole chronicle of the Snopes clan's taking over the hamlet of Frenchman's Bend and moving on to take over Jefferson, the county seat of Yoknapatawpha, Mississippi, and, by extension, the entire South in the twentieth century. For regional specificity, Faulkner has it all: from the overalled men sitting out on the bench in front of the general store, spitting tobacco juice as they comment on Flem Snopes's chicanery; to the importance of mules and horse-trading; to how "blacks, landed gentry, landless whites, yeoman whites, and newer generations" all talk, as Cleanth Brooks notes. For universals, we have everything from the husband's being driven to ruin himself just because his wife tells him not to ("Spotted Horses"); to the leaguing together to keep the devil one knows (Will Varner) in preference to the devil one does not know (Flem Snopes) in *The Hamlet;* to the high human comedy of trusting the truth of that which one obviously knows to be false, since the truth is too hard to deal with, as Buck and Buddy McCaslin ask no questions of their nominal slaves, free to roam from the unfinished plantation house all night so long as they are back behind the locked front door of the backless house by next morning (*Go Down, Moses*).

The writers of the Irish Literary Renaissance and the Southern Literary Renascence were cursed and blessed with provincial lives in insular Ireland and pen[almost]-insular life in the American South. A number of them fled, to seek a freer and ampler life elsewhere, always writing about the world fled, lovingly detailing it in all of its peculiarities. That the authors were themselves, the provincial Irish and Southerner, helped them to discover that these worlds, nicely observed, were the macrocosm. The South was the world; Ireland was the world.

Printed in the United States
By Bookmasters